Grammar Builder

A grammar guidebook for students of English

1

A. Amin

R. Eravelly

F.J. Ibrahim

CAMBRIDGE
UNIVERSITY PRESS

CAMBRIDGE UNIVERSITY PRESS
Cambridge, New York, Melbourne, Madrid, Cape Town, Singapore, São Paulo

Cambridge University Press
10 Hoe Chiang Road, #08-01/02 Keppel Towers, Singapore 089315

www.cambridge.org
Information on this title: www.cambridge.org/9780521548595

First published 2004
Third printing 2006

Printed in Singapore by Kyodo Printing Pte Ltd

Typeface Utopia. *System* QuarkXPress®

ISBN 0 521 54859 4 Grammar Builder Book 1
ISBN 0 521 54860 8 Grammar Builder Book 2
ISBN 0 521 54861 6 Grammar Builder Book 3
ISBN 0 521 54862 4 Grammar Builder Book 4
ISBN 0 521 54863 2 Grammar Builder Book 5

• INTRODUCTION •

To the student

This book is designed to help you master key concepts in English grammar easily and quickly. Students who need to take written exams as well as those who wish to write well will find the *Grammar Builder* series helpful.

You may use this book for self-study and practice. An Answers section is located at the back of the book.

To the teacher

The *Grammar Builder* series is a useful supplement to any main English language course and is suitable for both classroom teaching and self-study. The series focuses on written grammar and the key grammar concepts that students need to know for written exercises.

How the book is organised

The *Grammar Builder* series comprises five books for beginner to upper-intermediate level learners of British English. Books 1 and 2 are intended for learners who need to acquire the basics of grammar. Books 3 to 5 are for learners who need to strengthen their proficiency in grammar and improve their written English.

Each book is made up of 42 to 56 units, and units dealing with related topics (e.g. prepositions) are grouped together for ease of use.

A unit covers three to five grammar concepts and includes four to six different types of exercises. Key grammar concepts (e.g. tenses) taught in the lower level books are re-visited and expanded upon in the other books of this series. For a list of units, refer to the *Contents* at the beginning of each book.

The books use a simple but effective three-step approach (error identification, correction, and practice) to help learners master English grammar.

There are four pages per unit, and each unit is divided into three sections: *Checkpoint*, *Grammar Points*, and *Practice*.

All units begin with a *Checkpoint* section containing several pairs of numbered examples that show common grammatical errors and then their corrected forms. These examples of correct and incorrect usage demonstrate to the student how slight differences in expression can result in grammatical errors.

The students can then refer to the corresponding *Grammar Points* in the next section which explain the grammar concepts highlighted under *Checkpoint*, show how to apply the grammar concepts correctly, and provide more examples.

In the third section, *Practice*, students revise the grammar concepts they have learned by completing a group of exercises. (The answers can be found at the back of the book.) This enables quick revision of each concept, and allows students to see if there are any aspects that they do not fully comprehend. Students may review what they have learned by going through the *Grammar Points* again after completing each exercise. The *Grammar Points* can also be used for quick reference purposes.

There are six revision and evaluation tests towards the back of every book. These tests deal with most of the *Grammar Points* covered in each book.

CONTENTS

CONTENTS

UNIT 1.1 ARTICLES

a and an with singular nouns

Look at the **A** and **B** sentences below. Find out why **B** is correct and **A** is wrong in the **Grammar Points** section.

			GRAMMAR POINTS
1A	My brother goes to **an** university.	✗	
1B	My brother goes to **a** university.	✓	1
2A	**A** alligator is a reptile.	✗	
2B	**An** alligator is a reptile.	✓	2
3A	My aunt is **teacher**.	✗	
3B	My aunt is **a teacher**.	✓	3

GRAMMAR POINTS ─────────────────────────────────────

1 We use **a** with singular nouns which begin with consonant sounds.
(Consonants: b, c, d, f, g, h, j, k, l, m, n, p, q, r, s, t, v, w, x, y, z)
EXAMPLES: **a** book   **a** man
           a horse   **a** uniform (sounds like 'yu-niform')

2 We use **an** with singular nouns which begin with vowel sounds.
(Vowels: a, e, i, o, u)
EXAMPLES: **an** aeroplane   **an** hour (sounds like '-our')
           an exercise   **an** x-ray (sounds like 'ex-ray')

3 We use **a** or **an** when we speak of someone or something for the first time.
EXAMPLES: We saw **an** artist painting by the river.
            A stranger knocked at our door.

REMEMBER!

- The words **a**, **an** and **the** are called articles.

- A noun is the name of a person, an animal, a plant, a place or a thing.
  EXAMPLES: boy   tiger   tree   town   chair

- Words beginning with consonant letters do not always begin with consonant sounds. In the same way, words starting with vowel letters may not begin with vowel sounds.
  EXAMPLES: **an** honour (sounds like '-onour')
              a European (sounds like 'yu-ropean')

  Take note of the **sound** at the beginning of a word when choosing between the article **a** or **an**.

PRACTICE *A* Fill in the blanks with **a** or **an**.

1 _____ airport

2 _____ baton

3 _____ elephant

4 _____ flower

5 _____ hourglass

6 _____ iron

7 _____ racquet

8 _____ seed

9 _____ umpire

10 _____ woman

YOUR SCORE
10

PRACTICE *B* Fill in the blanks with **a** or **an**.

1 That's _____ UFO.

2 _____ ostrich is _____ bird.

3 Joseph wants to be _____ engineer.

4 This is not _____ ape. It is _____ gorilla.

5 There is _____ pond in Mary's garden.

6 John bought _____ atlas and _____ dictionary at _____ book fair.

YOUR SCORE
10

PRACTICE *C* Complete the table.

	a	**an**
1 animal	_c_ _o_ w	_a_ n _t_
2 bird	__ r __ w	__ a __ l e
3 building	__ c h __ o l	__ f f __ c e
4 flower	__ o s __	__ r c h __ d
5 food	__ a __ d w __ c h	__ c __ - c r __ a m
6 object	__ a __ n c o __ t	__ m b r __ l l __

YOUR SCORE
10

3

What do these people do? Fill in the blanks with **a** or **an** and the nouns in the box.

| accountant | inspector | journalist | lawyer | optician | singer |

Brian de Souza

Stella Jones

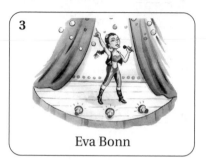

Eva Bonn

Martin Chan

Patrick Hill

Faizal Hussein

1 Brian de Souza is _a journalist._____

2 Stella Jones is _____

3 Eva Bonn is _____

4 Martin Chan is _____

5 Patrick Hill is _____

6 Faizal Hussein is _____

YOUR SCORE
10

PRACTICE $\boxed{E}$ Fill in the blanks with the words in the boxes.

1 Danny drew an _____ and a _____ in his sketchbook.

| igloo | tent |

2 We saw an _____ and a _____ on the stage .

| adult | child |

3 This pendant has both an _____ and a _____ in it.

| diamond | emerald |

4 That musician owns an _____ and a _____ .

| organ | ukelele |

5 I use a _____ to add numbers. Some people prefer to use an _____ .

| abacus | calculator |

YOUR SCORE

10

4

PRACTICE **F** Fill in the blanks with suitable words in the boxes. Each word may only be used once.

Occupation	Home	Nationality	Animal	Place
actor	apartment	Egyptian	hamster	cinema
vet	house	Mexican	owl	orchard

Meera is 13 years old. She is an (1) _____ . She and her family live in the countryside. They have a (2) _____ in an estate next to an (3) _____ . They have an (4) _____ for a pet. Meera wants to be a (5) _____ .

Pedro is 12 years old. He is a (6) _____ . He and his family live in the city. They have an (7) _____ in a building next to a (8) _____ . They have a (9) _____ for a pet. Pedro wants to be an (10) _____ .

YOUR SCORE
10

PRACTICE **G** Tick the correct words to complete the sentences.

1 I'm hungry. Please give me _____ .

☐ a ☐ burger
☐ an ☐ drink

2 The bathroom tap is leaking. Please call for _____ .

☐ a ☐ electrician
☐ an ☐ plumber

3 Is there _____ to the top floor? I'm tired of climbing the stairs.

☐ a ☐ elevator
☐ an ☐ taxi

4 My uncle is in hospital. He's going to have _____ on Friday.

☐ a ☐ doctor
☐ an ☐ operation

5 Oh dear! I'm on the wrong road and I can't make _____ .

☐ a ☐ entrance
☐ an ☐ U-turn

YOUR SCORE
10

UNIT 1.2 ARTICLES

a, an, the with singular nouns

Look at the **A** and **B** sentences below. Find out why **B** is correct and **A** is wrong in the **Grammar Points** section.

GRAMMAR
POINTS

1A	A letter arrived for you this morning. Anna says **a letter** is from England.	✗	
1B	A letter arrived for you this morning. Anna says **the letter** is from England.	✓	1
2A	Where is Nancy? She is in **a kitchen**.	✗	
2B	Where is Nancy? She is in **the kitchen**.	✓	2
3A	Tonight **a moon** is bright.	✗	
3B	Tonight **the moon** is bright.	✓	3
4A	It is **23rd of May**.	✗	
4B	It is **the 23rd of May**.	✓	4

GRAMMAR POINTS

1 We use **the** when a person, an animal, a plant, a place or a thing is mentioned a second time.
EXAMPLES: I bought **a** book this morning. I am now reading **the** book.
There is **a** spot on your collar. You can use lime and salt to remove **the** spot.

2 We use **the** when it is clear to the listener or reader which person, animal, plant, place or thing we are referring to.
EXAMPLES: **The** judge found him not guilty. (= the judge in charge of his trial)
I need to go to **the** bathroom.   (= the bathroom in this building)

3 We use **the** when there is only one such thing.
EXAMPLES: **The** Earth goes round **the** sun.
Dina's dream is to sail around **the** world.

4 We usually use **the** before ordinal numbers.
EXAMPLES: I live on **the** third floor.
My birthday is on **the** second of June.

REMEMBER!
- An ordinal number is a number like **first**, **second**, **third** or **fourth** which shows the position of something in a list of items.

PRACTICE A Fill in the blanks with **a**, **an** or **the**.

1 There is _____ owl on my roof. My cat is watching _____ owl with great interest.

2 There are dark clouds in _____ sky. We can't see _____ sun.

3 Don't stand at _____ door, Marina. You are blocking _____ way.

4 I gave my brother _____ xylophone for his birthday. Now he plays _____ xylophone every day.

5 Mr Ho is looking for _____ architect to design his house. _____ architect must be good.

PRACTICE B Fill in the blanks with **a**, **an** or **the**.

There is (1) _____ shopping mall on Hicks Street with five fast food outlets, two department stores, (2) _____ amusement centre and (3) _____ musical fountain. All (4) _____ shop units are occupied, but there is (5) _____ unit on (6) _____ ground floor next to (7) _____ musical fountain that is empty. This unit can be rented for $8,000 (8) _____ month. So far, only (9) _____ ice-cream cafe has shown interest in renting (10) _____ unit.

PRACTICE C Rewrite the sentences. Put **a**, **an** or **the** in the correct places.

1 Sea is calm today.

_____

2 Would you like ice cube in your drink?

_____

3 Lisa uses apron when she cooks.

_____

4 I have orange and pear. I'll keep orange. Who wants pear?

_____

_____

5 My father works in bank. He leaves house at 8.00 a.m. and arrives at office at 8.30 a.m.

_____

_____

PRACTICE D Complete the conversation with **a**, **an** or **the**.

A : Janice, (1) _____ bouquet of roses came for you just now.

B : Who is it from?

A : I don't know. (2) _____ man delivered (3) _____ bouquet. He didn't look like
(4) _____ florist. He wore (5) _____ uniform. He could be in the army. Oh yes, he also
handed me (6) _____ envelope for you. I left both (7) _____ bouquet and
(8) _____ envelope on your desk.

B : Let me see . . . He gave me (9) _____ card but there's no name on it. It just says
'Meet me at the restaurant on (10) _____ tenth floor of the Hilton Hotel'.

PRACTICE E Ten of the underlined articles are incorrect. Write the correct articles in the
boxes provided.

1   I had a dream last night.
<u>A</u> dream was very strange. I
found myself in <u>a</u> kitchen.
There was <u>the</u> robot in the
5   kitchen. <u>A</u> robot looked at me
and held up <u>a</u> egg. It broke the
egg and placed <u>a</u> yolk and the
egg white in <u>the</u> dish. After that
it placed the dish in <u>a</u> oven. Thirty
10   seconds later, it opened <u>the</u> oven
and pointed to what was inside.
I saw three dishes there. In <u>a</u> first
dish was a pancake. In <u>a</u> second
dish was <u>a</u> omelette. What was that
15   in the last dish? It was <u>the</u> eggplant!

The

8

Rewrite the paragraph. Put **a**, **an** or **the** in the correct places.

Fly is insect. Ant is insect too. There are more than million species of insects in world. Insects have six legs. Their bodies are divided into three parts. First part is head. Second part is thorax and third part is stomach.

A fly is an insect.

_____

_____

_____

_____

_____

_____

YOUR SCORE

10

PRACTICE *G* The articles **a**, **an** and **the** have been correctly used in 10 of the sentences below. Tick these sentences.

1
- **A** My father bought a grand piano.
- **B** My father bought an grand piano.
- **C** My father bought the grand piano.

2
- **A** The train station is quite far from here.
- **B** An train station is quite far from here.
- **C** A train station is quite far from here.

3
- **A** Jason has to attend a interview tomorrow.
- **B** Jason has to attend an interview tomorrow.
- **C** Jason has to attend the interview tomorrow.

4
- **A** The iguana is a member of the lizard family.
- **B** An iguana is a member of the lizard family.
- **C** A iguana is a member of the lizard family.

5
- **A** My office is on fifth floor of this building.
- **B** My office is on a fifth floor of this building.
- **C** My office is on the fifth floor of this building.

6
- **A** I live next to a playground and a playground is crowded every day.
- **B** I live next to a playground and the playground is crowded every day.
- **C** I live next to the playground and the playground is crowded every day.

YOUR SCORE

10

UNIT 1.3 **ARTICLES**

the with proper nouns

Look at the **A** and **B** sentences below. Find out why **B** is correct and **A** is wrong in the **Grammar Points** section.

			GRAMMAR POINTS
1A	There is a river called **Ganges** in India.	✗	
1B	There is a river called **the Ganges** in India.	✓	1a
2A	Mrs Chong works at **General Hospital**.	✗	
2B	Mrs Chong works at **the General Hospital**.	✓	1b
3A	**Kingdom of Thailand** is in Southeast Asia.	✗	
3B	**The Kingdom of Thailand** is in Southeast Asia.	✓	1c
4A	**United States** is a large country.	✗	
4B	**The United States** is a large country.	✓	1d

GRAMMAR POINTS

1   We use **the** before some proper nouns such as:

(a)   the names of oceans, rivers, seas and straits

   EXAMPLES: **the** Pacific Ocean
   the (River) Nile
   the Red Sea
   the Straits of Malacca

(b)   the names of most buildings, landmarks, monuments and natural wonders

   EXAMPLES: **the** Sheraton Hotel
   the Empire State Building
   the Taj Mahal
   the Grand Canyon

(c)   the names of places containing **of**

   EXAMPLES: **the** Republic **of** China
   the University **of** Manchester

(d)   the names of places ending in plural 's'

   EXAMPLES: **the** British Isles
   the Netherlands

REMEMBER!

- A proper noun is the special name given to one particular person, animal, plant, place or thing. It begins with a capital letter.

- The following are some proper nouns which do not use **the**:

   (a)   the names of continents
      EXAMPLES: Africa, Australia

   (b)   the names of most countries
      EXAMPLES: Belgium, Thailand

   (c)   the names of most towns and cities
      EXAMPLES: Tokyo, Nairobi

   (d)   the names of streets
      EXAMPLES: Orchard Road
         Oxford Street

   (e)   the names of people
      EXAMPLES: Norman
         Penny

PRACTICE **A** Put **the** in the correct places.

1 I have a guitar. My brother bought _____ guitar in _____ Spain.

2 I live in _____ Seattle. My house is near _____ Space Needle.

3 I will attend a conference in _____ Australia next month. _____ conference will be at _____ University of New South Wales.

4 _____ National Museum is on _____ Travers Road. It is next to _____ Regent Hotel.

PRACTICE **B** There are 10 incorrect uses of **the** in the paragraph below. Cross them out.

The Mediterranean Sea is connected to the Atlantic Ocean by the Straits of the Gibraltar. It is connected to the Red Sea by the Suez the Canal. Long ago, traders on their way to the Europe or the Asia passed through the Mediterranean Sea. They also used some of the cities along the Mediterranean the coast as trading centres. Constantinople in the Turkey, the Venice in the Italy and the Barcelona in the Spain were important cities to them.

PRACTICE **C** Fill in the blanks with **a**, **an**, **the** or **–** (no article). Then look up the answers to the quiz in an encyclopaedia.

QUIZ TIME

1 Where is _____ Sahara Desert?

2 What is _____ unicycle?

3 Who was _____ first man in space?

4 Where is _____ Buenos Aires?

5 When did Neil Armstrong land on _____ moon?

6 What separates _____ San Francisco Bay from _____ Pacific Ocean?

7 Who was the 16th President of _____ United States of America?

8 What is _____ emu?

9 How long is _____ River Nile?

PRACTICE D Fill in the blanks with **the** or **–** (no article).

What I want to do next year…

★ visit (1) _____ Great Pyramid in (2) _____ Egypt;

★ take a gondola ride on (3) _____ Grand Canal in (4) _____
Venice;

★ stroll along (5) _____ Oxford Street in (6) _____ London and
then take a bus to (7) _____ Tower of London;

★ spend a month in (8) _____ Turkey to visit places like (9) _____
Göreme Open Air Museum and (10) _____ Blue Mosque.

YOUR SCORE

10

PRACTICE E Tick the sentences that use **the** correctly.

1 The Netherlands is also called Holland.

2 Vasco da Gama sailed round Cape of Good Hope in 1497.

3 The Sydney Opera House is closed for repairs.

4 Sherlock Holmes lived on the Baker Street.

5 The Indian Ocean lies to the south of India.

6 London lies on the River Thames.

7 I saw Carol at National Museum yesterday.

8 We sailed Tasman Sea between Australia and the New Zealand.

9 The Great Wall of China is more than 2,000 km long.

10 The Africa is the second largest continent in the world.

YOUR SCORE

10

PRACTICE *F* Tick the correct boxes to complete the sentences.

1 Jakarta is the capital of

	Indonesia.
	Republic of Indonesia.

2

	Hong Kong	is located near
	The Hong Kong

	Tropic of Cancer.
	the Tropic of Cancer.

3

	Louvre	is the national art gallery and museum of
	The Lourve

	France.
	the France.

4 Kenya is bounded by

	Somalia	and
	the Somalia

	Indian Ocean	on the east.
	the Indian Ocean

5

	Maria Island	is in
	The Maria Island

	Tasman Sea	off the coast of
	the Tasman Sea

	Tasmania.
	the Tasmania.

YOUR SCORE
10

PRACTICE *G* Rewrite the paragraph and put **a**, **an** or **the** in the correct places.

Gettysburg is small town in Pennsylvania near Susquehanna River. Gettysburg is famous in the history of United States of America as place where important battle was fought during American Civil War. Battle lasted from 1st of July to 3rd July 1863 and there were many casualties. The Union Army defeated Confederate Army, but it was another two years before Confederate Army surrendered. Abraham Lincoln gave speech about democracy at Gettysburg and this speech is called Gettysburg Address.

_____

_____

_____

_____

_____

_____

_____

_____

_____

_____

_____

YOUR SCORE
10

UNIT 1.4 **ARTICLES**

with countable and uncountable nouns

Look at the **A** and **B** sentences below. Find out why **B** is correct and **A** is wrong in the **Grammar Points** section.

			GRAMMAR POINTS
1A	There is **a mud** everywhere!	✗	
1B	There is **mud** everywhere!	✓	1
2A	I cannot get **drop of water** from my tap.	✗	
2B	I cannot get **a drop of water** from my tap.	✓	2
3A	**Soap** in this dish smells of roses.	✗	
3B	**The soap** in this dish smells of roses.	✓	3

GRAMMAR POINTS

1 Some nouns can be counted and they are called countable nouns. Some nouns cannot be counted and they are called uncountable nouns. We use **a** or **an** only before countable nouns.

EXAMPLES:

Countable Nouns	**Uncountable Nouns**
cake	bread
drum	machinery
lawnmower	rain
leaf	soil
racquet	tennis

Sarah baked **a cake** for me.   My mother makes **bread**.
A leaf fell from the tree.   **Rain** can cause flooding.

2 We use **a** or **an** with uncountable nouns in this way:

a/an + countable noun + **of** + uncountable noun

EXAMPLES:

Allan drinks **a cup of tea** every morning.   Sheila bought **a loaf of bread**.

3   We use **the** with uncountable nouns when it is clear to the listener or reader which things we are referring to. We do not use **the** with uncountable nouns when we are talking in general.

EXAMPLES: **The rice** in this supermarket is cheap.
Rice is the staple food of Asians. (general)

PRACTICE A Fill in the blanks with **a**, **an**, **the** or **–** (no article).

1   We need ____–____ air to live, but _____ air in our cities is polluted.

2   Mr Lee had _____ plate of fried noodles for lunch. Mrs Lee had _____ bowl of soup.

3   _____ money in that box is mine, and _____ money on that table is yours.

4   Look! There is _____ snow on _____ ground. _____ snow makes the place look beautiful.

5   We own _____ acre of _____ land outside Melbourne.

PRACTICE B Tick the correct boxes to complete the sentences. There may be more than one answer for each question.

1
	–
	A
	The

water from this tap is very dirty.

2   You need to add
	a salt
	a pinch of salt
	salt

to the soup.

3   I would like
	a tea
	a cup of tea
	tea

without
	the milk,
	a milk,
	milk,

please.

4   Columbia grows
	the coffee.
	a coffee.
	coffee.

	The coffee
	A coffee
	Coffee

is exported to many countries.

5   There is
	–
	a
	the

dust all over
	–
	a
	the

furniture in this room.

PRACTICE **C** Circle the correct articles or **–** (no article) to complete the sentences.

1 Peel **a** / **an** onion and chop it.

2 **An** / **The** oil in the pan is warm.

3 I need **a** / **–** flour, **a** / **–** salt and **a** / **–** baking powder for the biscuits.

4 Cream together **a** / **an** tablespoon of butter and **a** / **–** cup of sugar.

5 Mix **a** / **an** ounce of milk for the batter.

6 **A** / **The** cinnamon in this bottle has a lovely smell.

7 Use **a** / **–** vanilla essence for the cake.

YOUR SCORE

10

PRACTICE **D** Mark with ⋏ wherever **a**, **an** or **the** is missing. Then write the missing articles in the boxes.

1 Gold is type of metal.

2 Pewter is made by mixing tin with lead.

3 My brother has pewter mug.

4 Bronze lamp in my sitting room is from India.

5 Bronze is alloy of copper and tin.

YOUR SCORE

10

PRACTICE **E** Complete the sentences with the countable and uncountable nouns in the boxes.

1 _____ is a _____ we all enjoy.

2 I bought a _____ and some _____ .

3 There was a _____ of _____ on the floor.

4 Sheena placed a _____ of _____ on the potter's wheel.

5 An _____ of _____ is missing from the shop.

game	tennis
lace	ribbon
blood	drop
clay	lump
clothing	item

YOUR SCORE

10

PRACTICE **F**   Rewrite the sentences that are not correct.

1 A porcelain was first made in China.
   Porcelain was first made in China. _____

2 Peter doesn't eat the meat. He is an vegetarian.

   _____

3 Did you use cheese for this pie?

   _____

4 Where is a tube of glue I bought yesterday?

   _____

5 I prefer a golf to a squash.

   _____

6 The doctor gave her medicine for her cough.

   _____

PRACTICE **G**   Fill in the blanks with the correct words in the box. Each item
may be used more than once.

petrol	a petrol attendant	a petrol station
the petrol	the petrol attendant	the petrol station
a can of petrol	a container	the bottom of the container
	the container	

One evening, our car ran out of (1) _____ *petrol* _____ while we were on a lonely road.

Dad remembered passing (2) _____ some distance back. I agreed

to walk to (3) _____ to buy (4) _____

for the car.

When I got there, I found (5) _____ quite run-down. I explained to

(6) _____ what had happened. He took quite a while to find

(7) _____ . Finally, he brought out a rusty one and filled it with petrol.

I carried (8) _____ carefully but after a few steps,

(9) _____ gave way and all (10) _____

spilt to the ground. I just stood there dumbfounded. (11) _____

rushed over and apologised to me. He gave me another container of petrol and he also

offered to drive me back to the car.

17

UNIT 2 **POSSESSIVES**

> ## apostrophe ('), apostrophe 's' ('s), **of**

Look at the **A** and **B** sentences below. Find out why **B** is correct and **A** is wrong in the **Grammar Points** section.

CHECKPOINT

				GRAMMAR POINTS
1A	My **cousins** wife is very kind.	✗		
1B	My **cousin's** wife is very kind.	✓		1
2A	**Mens'** suits are expensive.	✗		
2B	**Men's** suits are expensive.	✓		2
3A	The **house's roof** is leaking.	✗		
3B	The **roof of the house** is leaking.	✓		3
4A	**The dress of Hannah** is pretty.	✗		
4B	**Hannah's dress** is pretty.	✓		4

GRAMMAR POINTS

1 We usually add **'s** to a person or an animal to show ownership or relationship.

EXAMPLES: **Ownership**

Adam's football, the **girl's** jackets
the **sparrow's** nest, the **lion's** paws

Relationship

my **aunt's** friend, my **brother's** classmates
the **bulldog's** master, the **horse's** trainers

2 We usually add **'** to plural nouns ending in 's', and **'s** to plural nouns not ending in 's' to show ownership or relationship.

EXAMPLES: the **teachers'** notes   (singular – the **teacher's** notes)
the **children's** nanny (singular – the **child's** nanny)
the **sheep's** tails   (singular – the **sheep's** tail)

3 We usually use **of** to show relation or association with plants, places and objects.

EXAMPLES: the branches **of the tree**
the manager **of the factory**
the door **of the car**

> **REMEMBER!**
> ■ Sometimes, it is possible to use **'s** with plants, places and objects.
> EXAMPLE: the **country's** population

4 We do not usually use **of** with people.

EXAMPLES: the book **of my brother** ✗   the uncle **of Mr Lim** ✗

my brother's book ✓   **Mr Lim's** uncle ✓

18

PRACTICE $\boxed{A}$ Rewrite the sentences. Put **'s** or **'** in the correct places.

1 A giraffe neck is very long.

_____

2 The boys parents took them on holiday.

_____

3 Annas mother is a lawyer.

_____

4 The girls voices are excellent.

_____

5 She drew four elephants and painted the elephants trunks brown.

_____

6 Peter took his dogs to the vet. The vet checked the dogs ears.

_____

7 Rachel borrowed Jan dictionary yesterday.

_____

8 I bought a dress from the ladies department.

_____

9 The businessmen meeting is at the Orchid Hotel.

_____

10 The pony owner rode it round the field.

_____

YOUR SCORE

/10

PRACTICE $\boxed{B}$ Rewrite the sentences that are incorrect.

1 The windows of the house were painted blue.

_____

2 The essay of Jill is about her childhood.

_____

3 The book's writer is Alice King.

_____

4 My shoes heels are broken.

_____

5 The reindeer's antlers are enormous.

_____

YOUR SCORE

/10

This is Ricky's family tree. Use the diagram and the words in the boxes to make sentences.

| | man or boy |
| | woman or girl |

1 | Tim/Amy | — | husband |

Tim is Amy's husband.

2 | Liz/Tony | — | wife |

_____

3 | Roger and Liz/Tim | — | children |

_____

4 | Rose/Ben | — | ? |

_____

5 | Ricky and Mike/Winnie | — | ? |

_____

6 | Ben/Ricky | — | ? |

_____

YOUR SCORE 10

The underlined words contain a mistake. Rewrite the words in the boxes and correct the mistakes.

1 Eric grandparents live on Birch Street.

2 Jane has three aunts. Her aunts favourite hobby is horseriding.

3 The pet of David is a dwarf hamster.

4 The children often meet at Bill's house. They especially love to play in the house's basement.

5 That shop sells womens magazines.

6 The laughter of the students could be heard from the corridor.

7 The sister of my classmate is the president of the music club.

8 The tiger's cub looked at us through the cage's bars.

9 The policewomens' uniforms look smart. The design of the berets is so stylish.

10 My little cousins enjoyed the movie's funny parts but cried during the frightening scenes.

PRACTICE *E* Rewrite the possessive forms of the words in the brackets correctly.

Edna and Belle moved from the city to the countryside because they wanted to enjoy **1** (a small town's peace and quiet). Unfortunately, their peaceful lives were often disrupted by their neighbours. The Samson family next door had three guard dogs. At night, the **2** (dogs) barking often disturbed the two **3** (ladies) sleep. Their other neighbour, Mr Gopal, was a retired fireman. The **4** (smoke's smell) from the **5** (kitchen of the ladies) always sent him hurrying over to their rescue. When they explained that they had a smoky old stove, the former **6** (fireman) reply was: "Better safe than sorry." So he continued to rush to his **7** (neighbours) rescue each time.

One night, the ladies were awakened by barking sounds as usual but this time they saw smoke in their bedroom. They opened **8** (the room's window) to shout for help. Mr Gopal was already there with a ladder to help get them out.

Thanks to **9** (the Samsons) dogs and **10** (Mr Gopal) vigilance, the ladies were able to escape unharmed from the fire. After the incident, the Samsons and Mr Gopal became **11** (best friends of the ladies) in the neighbourhood.

1 *the peace and quiet of a small town*

2

3

4

5

6

7

8

9

10

11

UNIT 3.1 PERSONAL PRONOUNS AS SUBJECTS

Look at the **A** and **B** sentences below. Find out why **B** is correct and **A** is wrong in the **Grammar Points** section.

GRAMMAR POINTS

CH ECKPOINT

			GRAMMAR POINTS
1A	**The boy** likes animals. **The boy** has two cats and three rabbits.	✗	
1B	**The boy** likes animals. **He** has two cats and three rabbits.	✓	1
2A	I live in a block of flats. **They are** a high-rise building.	✗	
2B	I live in a block of flats. **It is** a high-rise building.	✓	2

GRAMMAR POINTS

1 Pronouns are words that take the place of nouns. We use a pronoun in place of a noun so that we do not have to repeat the noun.

EXAMPLE: Gina liked the roses. **She** put them in a vase. ✓

Gina liked the roses. Gina **she** put them in a vase. ✗

2 Singular pronouns replace singular nouns. Plural pronouns replace plural nouns.

EXAMPLE: The **lady** went to a party. **She** wore an elegant dress.
The **ladies** went to a party. **They** wore elegant dresses.

REMEMBER!

■ A personal pronoun can be the subject of a sentence (the subject is what the sentence is about). Personal pronouns as subjects of sentences are as follows:

	Singular	Plural
1st person (the speaker or speakers)	I	we
2nd person (the person or persons spoken to)	you	you
3rd person (the person or persons, thing or things spoken about)	he, she, it	they

PRACTICE $\boxed{A}$ Tick the correct boxes to complete the sentences.

1 Mr and Mrs Lee visited the museum.

	He
	They

went by bus.

2 Jenny and I like sweet things.

	We
	You

love to eat ice-cream.

3 You and Mark passed the test.

	They
	You

both scored 90 marks.

4 The bride is beautiful.

	He
	She

has a wonderful smile.

5 The sun is bright.

	He
	It

is high in the sky.

6 New York is a modern city.

	It
	They

has many tall buildings.

7 That waitress is very polite.

	She
	We

is also friendly.

8 The flowers are lovely.

	It
	They

also smell sweet.

9 Grandfather went for a walk.

	He
	She

went to the park.

10 Ralph bought a watch and a pen from the shop.

	It
	They

were quite expensive.

YOUR SCORE
10

PRACTICE $\boxed{B}$ Underline the correct pronouns.

1 The sheep are obedient. (It / They) obey the shepherd and (he / it) protects them from danger.

2 Mr Raj is coaching the footballers and (he / she) is good. (He / They) are playing well now.

3 You and I have the same hobbies. (I / We) am glad (we / you) are friends.

4 Mum has a rose plant. (It / She) waters the plant regularly so (it / she) is very healthy.

5 I am Dr Lim's patient. May (He / I) make an appointment, please? Is (he / you) free to see me at
   11 a.m. tomorrow?

YOUR SCORE
10

PRACTICE **C** Fill in the blanks with suitable pronouns to replace the underlined words.

1 I sat for a test. The test [ ] was quite difficult.

2 Bob does not play football. Bob [ ] prefers basketball.

3 India and China are large countries. India and China [ ] are located in Asia.

4 Miss Warren is a successful writer. Miss Warren [ ] works very hard.

5 Sam's sister is attractive. Sam's sister [ ] has many admirers.

6 Dad and I are freezing in this weather. Dad and I [ ] need thicker blankets.

7 Mickey has lost his hamster. Mickey [ ] is crying.

8 The men are here to pave the driveway. The men [ ] want to speak to you, Dad.

9 Joyce's drawing is wonderful. Joyce's drawing [ ] won the first prize.

10 The cubs are very active. The cubs [ ] are chasing one another.

YOUR SCORE
10

PRACTICE **D** Fill in the blanks with suitable pronouns.

1 Every morning, my mother and I get up early and _____ go for a morning walk.

2 Snakes are reptiles. _____ are cold-blooded.

3 Jeff's sister sings beautifully. _____ often sings at concerts.

4 My father jogs or plays tennis in the evening. _____ enjoys outdoor activities.

5 Thank you for the present, Jessie. _____ are very generous.

6 Gold and silver are valuable metals. _____ are used in the making of jewellery.

7 We stayed at a small hotel. _____ had a lovely garden.

8 Johann Strauss and Richard Wagner were famous composers. _____ lived more than a hundred years ago.

9 An amethyst is a precious stone. _____ is purple in colour.

10 Emily Brontë was an English novelist and poet of the 19th century. _____ wrote only one novel – *Wuthering Heights*.

YOUR SCORE
10

PRACTICE *E* Rewrite the sentences using suitable pronouns.

1 Jan and I like the design of the cottages. They think they are interesting.
   Jan and I like the design of the cottages. We think it is interesting.

2 Billy looked after all the animals in the pet zoo. Billy said it loved visitors.

   _____

3 You and Anne look unwell. She should see Dr Carlos. Dr Carlos is good.

   _____

4 Grandpa is talkative but Grandma is quiet. Grandpa says Grandma doesn't get a chance to talk.

   _____

   _____

5 One of the postmen in my hometown was excellent. They looked at envelopes with names but no addresses and knew where it should go.

   _____

   _____

6 You and I should take up gymnastics. They will be fun and I will get a lot of good exercise.

   _____

   _____

YOUR SCORE

/ 10

PRACTICE *F* Complete the conversation with suitable pronouns.

Ted : I see that you like reading. At what age did (1) ____*you*____ learn to read?

Lisa : At three, (2) _____ think. Mum and I read picture books together. (3) _____ had fun.

Ted : I learnt to read from an elder sister. (4) _____ gave me interesting reading lessons. Mum and Dad couldn't join in. (5) _____ were too busy.

Lisa : I was lucky. Dad brought home exciting books. (6) _____ and I both enjoyed those books.

Ted : Do (7) _____ still read together?

Lisa : Yes, in a different way. (8) _____ often read the same books and discuss them.

Ted : My sister and (9) _____ can't do that often now. (10) _____ lives very far from here. But we still love reading. (11) _____ is our favourite pastime.

YOUR SCORE

/ 10

UNIT 3.2 PERSONAL PRONOUNS AS SUBJECTS AND OBJECTS

Look at the **A** and **B** sentences below. Find out why **B** is correct and **A** is wrong in the **Grammar Points** section.

CHECKPOINT

1A	Sally and **me** went to the movies.	✗	
1B	Sally and **I** went to the movies.	✓	1
2A	**I and you** like the same food.	✗	
2B	**You and I** like the same food.	✓	2
3A	The visitor spoke to **me and Joseph**.	✗	
3B	The visitor spoke to **Joseph and me**.	✓	3

GRAMMAR POINTS

1 A personal pronoun can be the **subject** or the **object** of a sentence. The object is the person or thing that the subject does something to. Pronouns used as the subject of a sentence must be in the subjective form. Pronouns used as the object of a sentence must be in the objective form.

Subjective form	I	we	you	he	she	it	they
Objective form	me	us	you	him	her	it	them

EXAMPLES:

a  **I** chased a goose.   The goose chased **me**.

b  **We** watched a lion.   The lion watched **us**.

c   **You** like the dolphin.   The dolphin likes **you**.

d  **You** tickled the elephants.   The elephants tickled **you**.

26

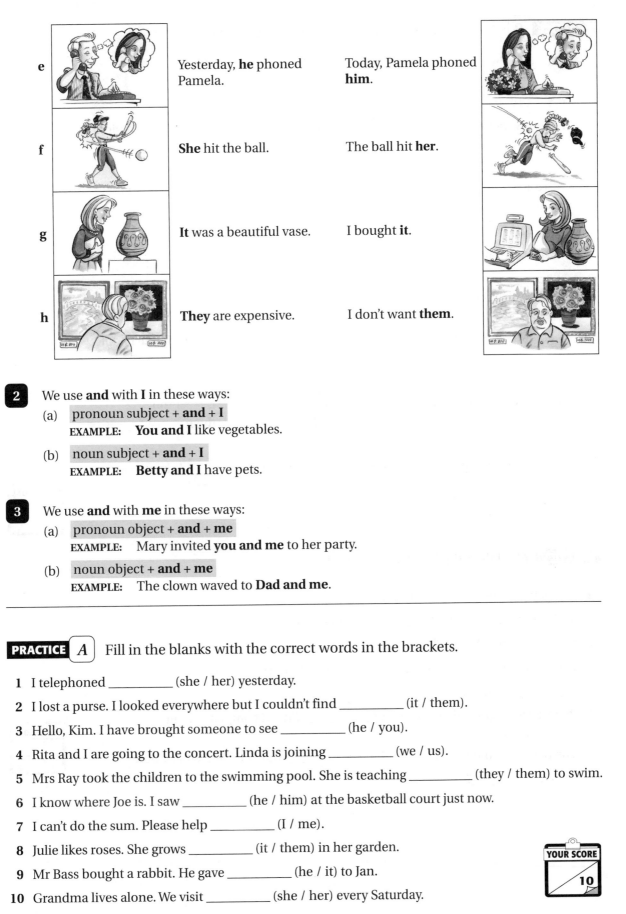

e	Yesterday, **he** phoned Pamela.	Today, Pamela phoned **him**.
f	**She** hit the ball.	The ball hit **her**.
g	**It** was a beautiful vase.	I bought **it**.
h	**They** are expensive.	I don't want **them**.

2 We use **and** with **I** in these ways:

(a) pronoun subject + **and** + **I**
EXAMPLE: **You and I** like vegetables.

(b) noun subject + **and** + **I**
EXAMPLE: **Betty and I** have pets.

3 We use **and** with **me** in these ways:

(a) pronoun object + **and** + **me**
EXAMPLE: Mary invited **you and me** to her party.

(b) noun object + **and** + **me**
EXAMPLE: The clown waved to **Dad and me**.

PRACTICE *A* Fill in the blanks with the correct words in the brackets.

1 I telephoned _____ (she / her) yesterday.

2 I lost a purse. I looked everywhere but I couldn't find _____ (it / them).

3 Hello, Kim. I have brought someone to see _____ (he / you).

4 Rita and I are going to the concert. Linda is joining _____ (we / us).

5 Mrs Ray took the children to the swimming pool. She is teaching _____ (they / them) to swim.

6 I know where Joe is. I saw _____ (he / him) at the basketball court just now.

7 I can't do the sum. Please help _____ (I / me).

8 Julie likes roses. She grows _____ (it / them) in her garden.

9 Mr Bass bought a rabbit. He gave _____ (he / it) to Jan.

10 Grandma lives alone. We visit _____ (she / her) every Saturday.

YOUR SCORE

10

1 Today is Emily's birthday. David sent $\boxed{\begin{array}{|c|} \hline \text{she} \\ \hline \text{her} \\ \hline \end{array}}$ a basket of flowers.

2 This is my friend Larry. $\boxed{\begin{array}{|c|} \hline \text{He} \\ \hline \text{Him} \\ \hline \end{array}}$ wants to join $\boxed{\begin{array}{|c|} \hline \text{we} \\ \hline \text{us} \\ \hline \end{array}}$ on the excursion.

3 Mrs Wells wants to see Fiona. $\boxed{\begin{array}{|c|} \hline \text{She} \\ \hline \text{Her} \\ \hline \end{array}}$ has found her purse.

4 The old man showed Jason and $\boxed{\begin{array}{|c|} \hline \text{me} \\ \hline \text{I} \\ \hline \end{array}}$ the secret door. $\boxed{\begin{array}{|c|} \hline \text{She} \\ \hline \text{It} \\ \hline \end{array}}$ was behind

a cupboard in the castle.

5 Mr and Mrs Tanaka are my neighbours. $\boxed{\begin{array}{|c|} \hline \text{They} \\ \hline \text{Them} \\ \hline \end{array}}$ are very considerate people.

6 Danny and Paul enjoy Chinese food. $\boxed{\begin{array}{|c|} \hline \text{I} \\ \hline \text{Me} \\ \hline \end{array}}$ like $\boxed{\begin{array}{|c|} \hline \text{it} \\ \hline \text{them} \\ \hline \end{array}}$ too.

7 I have walked along The Milford Track in New Zealand. $\boxed{\begin{array}{|c|} \hline \text{It} \\ \hline \text{Its} \\ \hline \end{array}}$ is known as

"the finest walk in the world".

YOUR SCORE
/ 10

PRACTICE $\boxed{C}$ Fill in the blanks with suitable pronouns.

1 The actress is ill. _____ needs a doctor.

2 Kathy and I are old friends. _____ come from the same town.

3 I want to go too, Mum. Please take _____ with _____ .

4 I don't buy bookmarks. I make _____ myself. Here's one bookmark I made.
_____ is for you.

5 Robert was angry with his sister but _____ did not complain about
_____ .

6 The bear moved towards Jerry and me. _____ were terrified. What would
it do to _____ ?

YOUR SCORE
/ 10

PRACTICE $\boxed{D}$ Circle the letters of the sentences which use pronouns **incorrectly**.

1 **(A)** The policeman advised me and Rose to go home.
 B The policeman advised Rose and me to go home.
 (C) The policeman advised Rose and I to go home.

2 **A** We like cartoons because they make us laugh.
 B We like cartoons because it makes us laugh.
 C We like cartoons because they make we laugh.

3 **A** Us girls told the boys that they should join the tennis club.
 B We girls told the boys that them should join the tennis club.
 C We girls told the boys that they should join the tennis club.

4 **A** Me and you have the same hobbies.
 B You and I have the same hobbies.
 C You and me have the same hobbies.

5 **A** The lifeguard smiled at the lady when she called he a hero.
 B The lifeguard smiled at the lady when her called him a hero.
 C The lifeguard smiled at the lady when she called him a hero.

6 **A** You and she must let us all help you.
 B You and she must let we all help you.
 C You and her must let us all help you.

YOUR SCORE
10

PRACTICE $\boxed{E}$ Fill in the blanks with suitable pronouns.

Dear Sue,

How are you? Mum and Dad miss (1) _____*you*_____ and so do Ken and (2) _____ . Dad says (3) _____ finds life dull without you around to tease (4) _____ . Mum says (5) _____ doesn't feel like singing because you aren't here to accompany (6) _____ on the piano.

Maths is tough without you to teach Ken and (7) _____ easy ways of solving problems. You also helped (8) _____ to love maths by making (9) _____ enjoyable.

Please write. Grandpa and Grandma say (10) _____ would like to hear from you too. (11) _____ all want to know about your adventures at the university.

Love,
Ben

YOUR SCORE
10

29

UNIT 3.3 POSSESSIVE ADJECTIVES AND POSSESSIVE PRONOUNS

Look at the **A** and **B** sentences below. Find out why **B** is correct and **A** is wrong in the **Grammar Points** section.

GRAMMAR
POINTS

1A	The small bag is **hers bag**.	✗	
1B	The small bag is **hers**.	✓	1
2A	The red umbrella is **your one**.	✗	
2B	The red umbrella is **yours**.	✓	2
3A	The cat hurt **it's** paw.	✗	
3B	The cat hurt **its** paw.	✓	3

GRAMMAR POINTS

1 We use possessive adjectives and possessive pronouns to show ownership or relationship. A possessive adjective goes together with a noun. A possessive pronoun takes the place of a possessive adjective and its noun.

EXAMPLES:　This is the children's tree house.　　　Kim is Mrs Lee's daughter.
　　　　　　　This is **their** tree house.　　　　　　Kim is **her** daughter.
　　　　　　　This tree house is **theirs**.　　　　　　Kate is my daughter and Kim is **hers**.

Personal pronouns (subjective form)	I	we	you	he	she	it	they
Possessive adjectives	my (book)	our (camera)	your (car)	his (pen)	her (bag)	its (paw)	their (toys)
Possessive pronouns	mine	ours	yours	his	hers	–	theirs

2 We do not use **one** after a possessive adjective.

EXAMPLE:　I parked my car next to **hers**. ✓

　　　　　　　I parked my car next to **her one**. ✗

3 We must not confuse **its** with **it's**.

(a) **Its** is a possessive adjective.
　　EXAMPLE:　The lioness is feeding **its** cubs.

(b) **It's** is the short form for **It is**.
　　EXAMPLES:　This is a flower. **It is** a rose.
　　　　　　　　　This is a flower. **It's** a rose.

REMEMBER!
- The possessive pronoun for **I** is **mine**, not **mines**.
- The personal pronoun **it** does not have a possessive pronoun form.

30

PRACTICE $\boxed{A}$ Tick the sentences that use possessive adjectives and possessive pronouns correctly.

1 ☐ **A** She father is a doctor.
  ☐ **B** Her father is a doctor.

2 ☐ **A** Those shirts are ours.
  ☐ **B** Those shirts are our.

3 ☐ **A** I know your brother.
  ☐ **B** I know yours brother.

4 ☐ **A** This car is he's.
  ☐ **B** This car is his.

5 ☐ **A** Tara's school is very far from my one.
  ☐ **B** Tara's school is very far from mine.

6 ☐ **A** Those letters are her ones.
  ☐ **B** Those letters are hers.

7 ☐ **A** The calculators are their.
  ☐ **B** The calculators are theirs.

8 ☐ **A** My friends are very helpful.
  ☐ **B** Mine friends are very helpful.

9 ☐ **A** The butterfly spread it's wings.
  ☐ **B** The butterfly spread its wings.

10 ☐ **A** Her puzzle is difficult.
   ☐ **B** Hers puzzle is difficult.

YOUR SCORE
10

PRACTICE $\boxed{B}$ Complete the conversation with the correct words in the brackets.

1 A: (1) _____ (you / your) leg is bleeding. What happened?

  B: (2) _____ (I / my) cat was sleeping and I did not see (3) _____ (he / it).

  I stepped on (4) _____ (it's / its) tail. Then I fell and hurt (5) _____ (mine / my) leg.

2 A: You and Nathan visited Sri Lanka and India last month. Did you enjoy (6) _____ (your / yours) trip?

  B: Yes. (7) _____ (we / our) stay in the two places was exciting. We learnt a lot about the people there, and (8) _____ (their / theirs) daily lives.

  A: Did you make a lot of friends?

  B: Yes, and (9) _____ (our / ours) relatives in India came to see

  (10) _____ (we / us) at the hotel. We had a wonderful time.

YOUR SCORE
10

31

PRACTICE $\boxed{C}$ Fill in the blanks with suitable possessive adjectives or possessive pronouns. Use the words in the boxes to help you.

1 My suitcase is very heavy. Anna, could I put some of _____*my*_____ things
   into _____*your*_____ bag? $\boxed{\text{I} \mid \text{you}}$

2 We checked in _____ luggage. Louise and Nigel haven't checked in
   _____. $\boxed{\text{we} \mid \text{they}}$

3 The air stewardess won't allow Mr Wilson to carry _____ golf bag onto the
   plane but he refuses to accept _____ ruling. $\boxed{\text{he} \mid \text{she}}$

4 Mona is at the Immigration Counter getting _____ passport checked. $\boxed{\text{she} \mid \text{we}}$
   Let's get _____ ready now.

5 Dad has our video camera on _____ shoulder. Where is _____, $\boxed{\text{he} \mid \text{you}}$
   Uncle Joe?

6 Dad and Mum have found _____ seats. I wonder which seat is _____. $\boxed{\text{they} \mid \text{I}}$

YOUR SCORE

10

PRACTICE $\boxed{D}$ Complete the conversation with suitable possessive adjectives or possessive pronouns. Use the words in the brackets to help you.

Julie : Look what I found in this old chest!

Betty : Hey, that's (1) _____*mine*_____ (Betty's). It's (2) _____ (Betty's) Olympic Games cap.

Julie : What about this T-shirt? Is it (3) _____ (Betty's) too?

Betty : Let me see. It could be John's. Yes, it is. The initials J.F. are (4) _____ (John's).

Julie : Oh! This poor doll was (5) _____ (Julie's) favourite. (6) _____ (the doll's) legs

           have come off. Look! Isn't this the boys' train set? It's in pieces. It was (7) _____ (the
           boys') favourite toy.

Betty : This science experiment set is (8) _____ (the boys') too. Do you remember the time

           when John and Jerry offered (9) _____ (Betty's and Julie's) friends and us the drinks
           they had mixed?

Julie : Yes! (10) _____ (Betty's) face turned blue and (11) _____ (Julie's) face turned
           green!

YOUR SCORE

10

32

Rewrite the sentences using possessive adjectives or possessive pronouns correctly.

1 I'll follow yours idea. If it doesn't succeed, I'll try mines.
   I'll follow your idea. If it doesn't succeed, I'll try mine.

2 The scouts put up theirs tents near our ones.

   _____

3 After finishing hers meal, she gives the hamster it's food.

   _____

4 He son's face is exactly like he face.

   _____

5 I'll wear this dress for me first party because I like it's colour.

   _____

6 The small room is your one and the big one is their.

   _____

YOUR SCORE
10

PRACTICE F Complete the passage with suitable possessive adjectives or possessive pronouns.

Next month, I will be moving to a new two-storey house with (1) _____my_____ parents. They will have (2) _____ bedroom and bathroom on the ground floor. In fact, almost the whole of that floor will be (3) _____ so they will decide on (4) _____ decor. Dad will have (5) _____ study and Mum will have (6) _____ art room.

I will have (7) _____ bedroom and a small TV area upstairs. Most of the living space on the upper floor will be (8) _____ .

I'm sure that the three of us will be happy in (9) _____ new home. Dad claims that the idea for it is (10) _____ . Mum just smiles because the idea is actually (11) _____ .

YOUR SCORE
10

UNIT 3.4 DEMONSTRATIVE ADJECTIVES AND DEMONSTRATIVE PRONOUNS

this, that, these, those

Look at the **A** and **B** sentences below. Find out why **B** is correct and **A** is wrong in the **Grammar Points** section.

			GRAMMAR POINTS
1A	**That** men are hardworking.	✗	
1B	**Those** men are hardworking.	✓	1
2A	**This** mountain is very far from here.	✗	
2B	**That** mountain is very far from here.	✓	2

1 We use **this** and **that** with singular nouns. We use **these** and **those** with plural nouns.
EXAMPLES: **this** athlete – **these** athletes   **that** shop – **those** shops

2 We use **this** and **these** to point to people and things that are near us.
We use **that** and **those** to point to people and things that are far from us.
EXAMPLES:

REMEMBER!
- **This**, **that**, **these** and **those** point to specific people or things.

  EXAMPLES: **Kittens** are playful.   (not pointing to specific kittens)
  Those kittens are playful.   (pointing to specific kittens)

34

■ **This**, **that**, **these** and **those** are demonstrative adjectives when they are followed by nouns and demonstrative pronouns when they are not followed by nouns.

EXAMPLES: This table is small.   This is a small table.

demonstrative adjective   noun   demonstrative pronoun

PRACTICE *A*   Tick the correct boxes to complete the sentences.

1 ☐ That / ☐ Those   boxes are full of apples.

2 ☐ This / ☐ Those   dress is well-made.

3 ☐ That / ☐ Those   is a hippopotamus.

4 ☐ This / ☐ These   are roses.

5 ☐ This / ☐ These   are not lillies.   ☐ That / ☐ Those   are lillies.

6 I have ☐ this / ☐ those   book. I haven't got ☐ that / ☐ these   book.

7 I want some of ☐ this / ☐ these   grapes and some of ☐ that / ☐ those   apples.

YOUR SCORE

/10

PRACTICE *B*   Rewrite the sentences without changing the meaning. Use demonstrative pronouns and demonstrative adjectives.

1 This is a pretty blouse.
   This blouse is pretty.

2 Those are fat hens.

3 These are sweet apples.

4 This book is heavy.

5 That hornbill is beautiful.

YOUR SCORE

6 That is a modern building.

/10

35

PRACTICE *C* Write sentences using **this**, **that**, **these** or **those** and the words in the pictures.

1 trapeze artists

Those are trapeze artists.

2 jugglers

3 a clown

4 the lion trainer

5 an acrobat

6 the lion

YOUR SCORE

10

PRACTICE *D* Underline the correct words in the brackets to complete the conversation.

Shirley : Where shall I hang **1** (<u>this</u> / that) picture, Mum?

Mum : **2** (This / That) is a lovely picture you're holding, Shirley. Let's hang it on

3 (that / those) wall.

Shirley : Shall I put **4** (this / these) porcelain dolls on **5** (these / those) shelves over there?

36

Mum	:	Yes, but be careful. **6** (That / Those) are family heirlooms.
Shirley	:	Don't worry. **7** (These / Those) dolls are in safe hands.
Mum	:	Shirley, come over here and look at **8** (this / that).
Shirley	:	Who's the baby in **9** (this / these) photo, Mum?
Mum	:	It's you.
Shirley	:	**10** (This / These) can't be me!
Mum	:	It is you. Look at **11** (that / those) eyes.
Shirley	:	You're right. They do look like my eyes.

PRACTICE *E* Rewrite the incorrect sentences.

1 This building across the road is an art gallery.
   That building across the road is an art gallery. _____

2 You won't find jewels that are lovelier than these.

   _____

3 All these furniture here must be dusted.

   _____

4 This hill we are standing on is not very high. Those are much higher.

   _____

5 These pair of shoes are more stylish than the others.

   _____

6 Look at this out there in the field!

   _____

PRACTICE *F* Fill in the blanks with **this**, **that**, **these** or **those**.

(1) _____ planet that we live on is called Earth. Some of (2) _____ stars that you see in the sky are actually planets.

Do you recognise (3) _____ instrument I'm holding? Yes, (4) _____ is a telescope. It's an old-fashioned one, like (5) _____ used by people of the last century to look at the stars and the planets. Nowadays, astronomers use more powerful telescopes.

However, (6) _____ is not a bad instrument. Using one of (7) _____ , you can see quite a lot. Let's go outside. First, let's look at the sky without using the telescope. Can you see (8) _____ three stars in a row? Does anyone know what (9) _____ are called? Yes, Orion's belt. Hey! What's (10) _____ near Orion's belt? I've never seen it before!

UNIT 4 GENDER

Look at the **A** and **B** sentences below. Find out why **B** is correct and **A** is wrong in the **Grammar Points** section.

<table>
<tr><td></td><td></td><td></td><td>GRAMMAR
POINTS</td></tr>
<tr><td>1A</td><td>A lady visited us yesterday. He was Pam's friend.</td><td>✗</td><td></td></tr>
<tr><td>1B</td><td>A lady visited us yesterday. She was Pam's friend.</td><td>✓</td><td>1</td></tr>
<tr><td>2A</td><td>The lioness was so graceful we all watched it.</td><td>✗</td><td></td></tr>
<tr><td>2B</td><td>The lioness was so graceful we all watched her.</td><td>✓</td><td>2</td></tr>
</table>

GRAMMAR POINTS

1

(a) We use the pronouns **he, him, his** with singular masculine nouns referring to human beings.
EXAMPLES: king, man, son, waiter

(b) We use the pronouns **she, her, hers** with singular feminine nouns referring to human beings.
EXAMPLES: queen, woman, daughter, waitress

> **REMEMBER!**
> ■ Gender in English grammar refers to the division of nouns into feminine (female living things), masculine (male living things) and neuter (animals, plants and non-living things).

(c) We use the pronouns **it** and **its** with singular nouns referring to animals, plants and non-living things.
EXAMPLES: butterfly, rabbit, house, stone

(d) We use the pronouns **they**, **them**, **theirs** with plural nouns referring to living and non-living things.
EXAMPLES: women, waiters, rabbits, houses

2
We normally use the pronoun **it** when referring to an animal. However, we can also use **he, him, his**, or **she, her, hers** when we think of the animal as a person.
EXAMPLES: I can see a cockroach. **It** is behind you.
My puppy is called Jaffa. **He** likes to play with my shoes.

PRACTICE *A* Fill in the blanks with the correct words in the brackets.

1 My sister has a bicycle. _____ (He / She) cleans _____ (her / it) every weekend.

2 Alan saw two lizards. _____ (He / It) tried to catch _____ (it / them).

3 I saw a male _____ (gorilla / rooster) and a female _____ (elephant / lioness) at the zoo.

4 The people rolled out a red carpet for the king. _____ (He / It) walked on _____ (them / it).

5 The hungry wolf asked the little lamb where she was going. _____ (He / It)

was actually planning to eat _____ (she / her) up.

YOUR SCORE

10

38

PRACTICE *B*   Underline the words in the box that are either masculine or feminine.

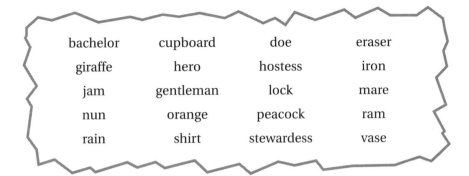

bachelor	cupboard	doe	eraser
giraffe	hero	hostess	iron
jam	gentleman	lock	mare
nun	orange	peacock	ram
rain	shirt	stewardess	vase

PRACTICE *C*   Write the words you underlined in *B* above in the columns below.

Masculine
1 _____
2 _____
3 _____
4 _____
5 _____

Feminine
1 _____
2 _____
3 _____
4 _____
5 _____

PRACTICE *D*   Fill in the blanks with correct pronouns.

1 Mr Shane is very kind. _____ always helps poor people.

2 A cobra is a snake. _____ is a dangerous animal.

3 Julia is a talented actress. I like _____ .

4 My uncle and aunt are here. _____ want to take me out.

5 The Planetarium is on that hill. _____ is open from 10 a.m. to 4 p.m.

6 The thieves ran very fast. We could not catch _____ .

7 John rescued the kitten trapped in the tree. Mrs Daniel thanked _____ .

8 The little boy is angry because his sister's toy is better than _____ .

9 Mary says this book is _____ . Please give it back to her.

10 It was Justin's birthday. Anna bought _____ a CD.

PRACTICE E Fill in the blanks with suitable words in the boxes.

1 _____ is here. She wants to see your parents.

2 _____ is an air steward.

3 The _____ ran after her cubs.

4 _____ is nervous. He has to give away the bride.

5 Mr Ito is our History teacher.

   _____ lessons are always interesting.

6 My friend's _____ lent me his bicycle.

7 Jason's _____ is sad. She misses her grandchildren.

8 The _____ told Sue he would give her the prize.

9 The _____ told her guards to pull up the drawbridge.

10 The _____ did her best to please the fussy customer.

Mr Chang	Miss Chang
my brother	my sister
lion	lioness
my father	my mother
her	his
nephew	niece
father-in-law	mother-in-law
head boy	head girl
prince	princess
salesgirl	salesman

YOUR SCORE 10

PRACTICE F Circle the words in the box that match the underlined words.

1 <u>She</u> is my father's sister.

2 <u>He</u> took the orders on a piece of paper.

3 <u>She</u> stopped the driver and gave him a ticket.

4 <u>He</u> put a diamond ring on her finger.

5 <u>Her</u> words struck fear into the villagers.

6 <u>He</u> promised to take care of her.

7 <u>His</u> performance on stage was superb.

8 This <u>lady</u> ruled the kingdom for a long period.

9 <u>She</u> raised all six children on her own.

10 The <u>man</u> demanded two months' rent from the tenant.

my aunt	my uncle
the waiter	the waitress
the policeman	the policewoman
the bride	the bridegroom
the witch's	the wizard's
her fiancé	his fiancée
the actor's	the actress's
the emperor	the empress
the widow	the widower
the landlady	the landlord

YOUR SCORE 10

40

PRACTICE *G*   Fill in the blanks with suitable words in the box.

brothers	girl	husband	man	nephews
niece	sister	him	it	them

After school, I sometimes babysit for my older (1) _____ Lucy. She has two sons and a daughter. Lena, the (2) _____ , is seven years old. Her (3) _____ , Mark and Matthew, are five and three.

Lucy is firm with the children but her (4) _____ isn't. He is a busy (5) _____ and seldom finds time to play with (6) _____ .

Babysitting for Lucy requires a lot of patience. My (7) _____ is talkative and my (8) _____ are naughty. Their puppy Sheba is naughty too. Just last week (9) _____ chewed up my sandals. Yesterday, Sheba chased the postman down the road and tried to bite (10) _____ .

YOUR SCORE

10

PRACTICE *H*   Underline the correct words to complete the passage.

I share a three-bedroom flat with two **1** (brother / sisters). The flat is small but cosy. **2** (He / It) is located on the second floor of an apartment block. We like it because it has **3** (his / its) own private stairway and entrance.

Our **4** (landlord / landlady) is Mrs Jenkins. She is a tall, well-built **5** (man / woman) with twinkling eyes and a warm smile. She lives on the ground floor with her **6** (husband / wife) and two sons.

The **7** (girls / boys) come up to our flat sometimes to deliver cakes and pies which their **8** (father / mother) has just baked. She is happy when we tell her how much we enjoy **9** (her / his) cooking. We have nothing to give her in return. Instead, we run errands for her and offer her sons help with their homework whenever they need **10** (him / it).

YOUR SCORE

10

UNIT 5.1 ADJECTIVES

> before nouns and after verbs

Look at the **A** and **B** sentences below. Find out why **B** is correct and **A** is wrong in the **Grammar Points** section.

CHECKPOINT

				GRAMMAR POINTS
1A	My car **is small car**.	✗		
1B	My car **is small**.	✓	1	
2A	Jasmine bought a **pink large** T-shirt.	✗		
2B	Jasmine bought a **large pink** T-shirt.	✓	2	
3A	Aisha has a **black white** dress.	✗		
3B	Aisha has a **black and white** dress.	✓	3	

GRAMMAR POINTS

1 We usually place an adjective before a noun **or** after the verb 'to be'.

EXAMPLES: You have a **large** house. ✓
noun

Your house is **large**. ✓
verb

Your house is **large** house. ✗
verb   noun

> **REMEMBER!**
> - An adjective describes a person, an animal, a plant, a place or a thing.
>
>   EXAMPLE: The clown has a **huge nose**.
>   adjective noun
>
> - The following are different forms of the verb 'to be':
>   **am, is, are, was, were, shall be, will be**

2 Size and colour are two groups of adjectives which we use very commonly. When we use both before a noun, we follow this order and do not use a comma or **and**:

1	2
SIZE	COLOUR
big	yellow
tiny	white

EXAMPLES: There is a **big yellow** hat on the shelf.
There is a **tiny white** pearl in this oyster.

3 When we use two adjectives from the colour group, we place **and** between them. We can use the adjectives in any order.

EXAMPLES: Her shoes are **black and brown**.
Her shoes are **brown and black**.

> **REMEMBER!**
> - The word **colour** is not used after a colour adjective.
>
>   EXAMPLE:
>
>   the **red colour** book ✗
>
>   the **red** book ✓

PRACTICE $\boxed{A}$ Complete the sentences with the words in the boxes. Use **and** where needed.

1 The birds are eating those _____*big red cherries*_____ .

big	cherries	red

2 The _____ belongs to my uncle.

purple	small	van

3 I found my _____ today.

black	handbag	orange

4 My ring has _____ .

blue	stones	tiny

5 That _____ is a bear.

animal	huge	brown

6 The _____ belongs to Brandon.

green	house	white

7 Kathy has a _____ .

grey	large	umbrella

8 Tina's sweater is _____ .

black	green

9 I'm making a _____ for the costume party.

huge	mask	purple

10 Mr Ford's yacht is _____ .

red	white

11 Your hockey stick is behind the _____
_____ .

brown	cupboard	small

YOUR SCORE
10

PRACTICE $\boxed{B}$ Some of the sentences below need **and**. Mark with λ wherever **and** is missing.

1 She put up the blue$_\lambda$green curtains.

2 There is a small blue bird in the nest.

3 Sam found your purple file.

4 I like those orange grey cushions.

5 Stephanie bought a brown black belt.

6 This castle has large white gates.

7 We saw a yellow black snake at the zoo.

8 I can see a big green apple on your tree.

9 The grey white building belongs to our company.

10 She put her ring into a small red box.

11 Let's buy this orange brown wrapping paper.

YOUR SCORE
10

PRACTICE **C** Tick the sentences that use the adjectives in the box correctly. There may be more than one answer for each question.

1 That coat belongs to my uncle.
- **A** That large brown coat belongs to my uncle.
- **B** That large and brown coat belongs to my uncle.
- **C** That brown large coat belongs to my uncle.

brown
large

2 The boxes are in the lorry.
- **A** The huge white boxes are in the lorry.
- **B** The huge boxes are in the white lorry.
- **C** The white boxes are in the huge lorry.

huge
white

3 There are ants on that fruit tree.
- **A** There are red tiny ants on that fruit tree.
- **B** There are tiny red ants on that fruit tree.
- **C** There are red ants on that fruit tiny tree.

red
tiny

4 I found a wallet in the bus.
- **A** I found a blue black wallet in the bus.
- **B** I found a blue and black wallet in the bus.
- **C** I found a black and blue wallet in the bus.

black
blue

5 The mobile phone is Allie's.
- **A** The yellow small mobile phone is Allie's.
- **B** The small, yellow mobile phone is Allie's.
- **C** The small yellow mobile phone is Allie's.

small
yellow

6 I like those shoes.
- **A** I like those red and white shoes.
- **B** I like those white and red shoes.
- **C** I like those red, white shoes.

red
white

YOUR SCORE
/10

PRACTICE **D** Underline the correct words to complete the passage.

Larry's dream car is a **1** (expensive / luxurious) sports car. It has a **2** (long red body / long and red body). The tyres, bumpers and sunroof are all **3** (black colour / black). The emblem on the bonnet is a **4** (golden tiny / tiny golden) hawk.

The interior of the car is **5** (space / spacious). It is carpeted with **6** (grey and brown / grey, brown) fabric. The seats are covered with **7** (shine / shiny) leather. An **8** (extra / large) compartment behind the front seats contains a **9** (silver slim / slim silver) television set and a **10** (advanced / sophisticated) computer.

YOUR SCORE
/10

PRACTICE E Rearrange the words to form correct sentences.

1 I — grey — kitten — like — that.
I like that grey kitten.

2 a — drives — Sam — small — truck.

3 and — balloon — blue — is — my — pink.

4 apples — are — big — these.

5 a — and — box — green — have — I — pencil — red.

6 are — earrings — huge — Mary's.

YOUR SCORE
10

PRACTICE F Rewrite the sentences so that the adjectives come after the verb 'to be'.

1 I have a brown bag.
My bag is brown.

2 This is an expensive ring.

3 Joe has a large TV set.

4 That is a tiny insect.

5 Michael has a red and black baseball cap.

6 There are small fish in this pond.

YOUR SCORE
10

45

UNIT 5.2 ADJECTIVES OF COMPARISON

Look at the **A** and **B** sentences below. Find out why **B** is correct and **A** is wrong in the **Grammar Points** section.

			GRAMMAR POINTS
1A	Anita is the **quieter** of the four sisters.	✗	
1B	Anita is the **quietest** of the four sisters.	✓	1
2A	Tom's computer is **more new** than mine.	✗	
2B	Tom's computer is **newer** than mine.	✓	2a
3A	I have the **wonderfullest** mother in the world.	✗	
3B	I have the **most wonderful** mother in the world.	✓	2b
4A	Lucy is **more carefuller** than Diana.	✗	
4B	Lucy is **more careful** than Diana.	✓	2c

GRAMMAR POINTS

1 When we compare two nouns, we use comparative adjectives. When we compare more than two nouns, we use superlative adjectives.

EXAMPLES: **tall:**   Joe is **taller** than John. (comparative adjective)
Richard is the **tallest** of the three brothers. (superlative adjective)

generous: Janet is **more generous** than Julie. (comparative adjective)
Sheila is the **most generous** of the three sisters. (superlative adjective)

2 (a) With one-syllable adjectives and some two-syllable adjectives, we usually use 'er' and 'est' endings for their comparative and superlative forms.

EXAMPLES: **bright:** The dining room is **brighter** than the kitchen.
The living room is the **brightest** room in the house.

pretty: Mrs Ford is **prettier** than her sister.
Carrie is the **prettiest** girl in class.

(b) With some two-syllable adjectives, adjectives with three or more syllables, and adjectives ending in 'ful', we use **more** and **most** for their comparative and superlative forms.

EXAMPLES: **handsome:** Bill is **more handsome** than Ivan.
Steve is the **most handsome** singer among the trio.

intelligent: Anne is **more intelligent** than Jane.
Marie is the **most intelligent** of the three.

forgetful: Arul is **more forgetful** than his brother.
He is the **most forgetful** boy in class.

(c) Since the 'er' ending and **more** are both forms of comparative adjectives, we cannot use them together.

46

Since the 'est' ending and **most** are both forms of superlative adjectives, we cannot use them together.

> **REMEMBER!**
> ■ The spelling of some adjectives needs to be changed before 'er' or 'est' can be added.
>
> | Adjective ending in 'e' ('e̷' + 'er'/'est') | Adjective ending in 'y' ('y̷' 'i' + 'er'/'est') | One-syllable adjective ending in a consonant (+ same consonant + 'er'/'est') |
> | --- | --- | --- |
> | (a) gentle → gentler, gentlest | (b) dirty → dirtier, dirtiest | (c) hot → hotter, hottest |

PRACTICE *A*   Fill in the blanks with the correct forms of the adjectives in the brackets.

1 Marie is _____*cleverer*_____ (clever) than Rita.

2 Ronnie is _____ (talkative) than his brother.

3 The tiger is the _____ (dangerous) animal in the zoo.

4 Silk is _____ (fine) than cotton.

5 The chicken curry was the _____ (taste) dish in the buffet.

6 Roy is _____ (strong) than Dan.

7 The second sum is _____ (difficult) than the first.

8 Neil is _____ (thin) than his father.

9 The _____ (thick) book in my schoolbag is this dictionary.

10 This is the _____ (popular) movie of the week.

11 The guest arrived _____ (early) than the host.

YOUR SCORE
10

PRACTICE *B*   Rearrange the words to form correct sentences.

1 dog — fiercer — is — Jerry's — mine — than.
   Jerry's dog is fiercer than mine.

2 is — Julie — of — sisters — tidiest — the — the.
   _____

3 Chris — have — I — interesting — more — games — than.
   _____

4 among — hardworking — Hillary — is — most — the — us.
   _____

5 aquarium — expensive — is — mine — more — than — your.
   _____

6 friendliest — in — is — man — Mark — my — neighbourhood — the.
   _____

YOUR SCORE
10

47

Globe Hotel
Room Rates
Single: $30
Double: $45

Lakeside Hotel
Room Rates
Single: $150
Double: $170

Imperial Hotel
Room Rates
Single: $120
Double: $140

1 (cheap / expensive)

The Imperial Hotel offers _____ accommodation than the Lakeside Hotel.

The Globe Hotel offers _____ accommodation among the three hotels.

Globe Hotel

Lakeside Hotel

Imperial Hotel

2 (luxurious / simple)

The bedrooms in the Lakeside Hotel are _____ than those in the Globe Hotel.

The bedrooms in the Imperial Hotel are _____ among the three hotels.

3 (far / near)

The Imperial Hotel is _____ to the city than the Lakeside Hotel.

The Globe Hotel is _____ to the city among the three hotels.

Globe Hotel

Lakeside Hotel

Imperial Hotel

4 (noisy / peaceful)

The Imperial Hotel has _____ surroundings than the Globe Hotel.

The Lakeside Hotel has _____ surroundings among the three hotels.

Globe Hotel	Lakeside Hotel	Imperial Hotel
Programme:	Programme:	Programme:
tours to the planetarium, House of Wax, Lobo's Farm, etc.	trip to a waterfall, jungle trekking	card game, folk dance

5 (boring / interesting)

The Lakeside Hotel has a _____ programme than the Imperial Hotel.

The Globe Hotel has _____ programme among the three hotels.

YOUR SCORE
10

PRACTICE | **D** | Compare the two ladies. Make sentences with the correct forms of the adjectives given.

1 slim

Beth is slimmer than Maggie.

2 elegant

_____

3 young

_____

4 tall

_____

5 cheerful

_____

6 neat

_____

Beth   Maggie

YOUR SCORE
10

PRACTICE | **E** | Complete the dialogues with the correct forms of the adjectives in the brackets. You will also need to use **than** or **the**.

A James : I'm sure I'm (1) _____ (fast) cyclist in school. Would anyone like to race against me?

Mark : I think I'm (2) _____ (fast) you, James. I'll race against you but

not here. This is (3) _____ (busy) road in town.

B Liz : This is (4) _____ (terrible) chicken soup I have ever tasted.

Mary : I know a restaurant that makes (5) _____ (good) chicken soup in this town.

Liz : Well, I'm sure any other chef can make chicken soup that is

(6) _____ (tasty) this!

Mary : That restaurant also has desserts that are (7) _____ (delicious) the ones here. I'll take you there next week.

C Roger : Is your new boss (8) _____ (efficient) the old one?

Dave : Oh yes! He's also (9) _____ (kind) my old boss. In fact he's

(10) _____ (understanding) boss I've ever had.

YOUR SCORE
10

49

UNIT 6 ADVERBS

Look at the **A** and **B** sentences below. Find out why **B** is correct and **A** is wrong in the **Grammar Points** section.

GRAMMAR POINTS

CHECKPOINT

1A	She writes **clear**.	✗	
1B	She writes **clearly**.	✓	1
2A	He drives **fastly**.	✗	
2B	He drives **fast**.	✓	2
3A	Leela took **slowly** her medicine.	✗	
3B	**Slowly** Leela took her medicine.	✓	
	Leela took her medicine **slowly**.	✓	3
	Leela **slowly** took her medicine.	✓	

GRAMMAR POINTS

1 We do not use adjectives to describe verbs. We use adverbs. Most adverbs are formed by adding the 'ly' ending to adjectives.

Adjectives	Adverbs (+ 'ly')	Adverbs ('y' 'i' + 'ly')
busy	–	busily
clumsy	–	clumsily
eager	eagerly	–
free	freely	–

EXAMPLES:

Jay played **badly** in the hockey match.
verb   _adverb_

The van driver shouted **angrily** at the cyclist.
verb   _adverb_

REMEMBER!

■ Adverbs are words which tell us more about verbs, adjectives or other adverbs. Adverbs are usually placed next to the words they describe.

(a) **adverbs with verbs**
EXAMPLE:
verb   adverb
He listens carefully to the commentator.

(b) **adverbs with adjectives**
EXAMPLE:
adverb   adjective
This house is quite big.

(c) **adverbs with other adverbs**
EXAMPLE:
adverb   adverb
They entered the house very quietly.

2 Some adverbs do not take the 'ly' ending. They have the same form as adjectives.

EXAMPLES:

far	fast	hard	last	long	straight

Mr Clarke was the **last** speaker.   (adjective)
Mr Clarke spoke **last**.   (adverb)

3 When the sentence has an object, we cannot place an adverb between the verb and its object.

EXAMPLES: He climbed quickly the tree.   ☒

verb   adverb   object

> **REMEMBER!**
> ■ The object in a sentence is the person or thing that receives the action done by the subject.

Quickly he climbed the tree. (adverb at the beginning of a sentence)   ✓

He climbed the tree **quickly**. (adverb at the end of a sentence)   ✓

He **quickly** climbed the tree. (adverb between the subject and the verb)   ✓

PRACTICE *A*   There are 10 adverbs in the box. Underline them.

attractive	better	early	efficient	excitedly	honest
hard	jealous	kindly	loving	quietly	rich
strangely	sweet	tenderly	thankful	tightly	warmly

YOUR SCORE
10

PRACTICE *B*   Fill in the blanks with the words in the brackets. Add 'ly' endings to the words where needed.

1 The young boy ate the burger _____ . (hungry)

2 It rained _____ this morning. (heavy)

3 The injured deer cannot walk _____ . (far)

4 Mrs Singh spoke _____ . (loud)

5 He went _____ to the station. (alone)

6 We will not stay _____ in Melbourne. (long)

7 They walked _____ across the hall. (silent)

8 The baby cries for food _____ . (frequent)

9 Crabs do not walk _____ . (straight)

10 They arrived _____ for the wedding. (late)

YOUR SCORE
10

PRACTICE $\boxed{C}$ Mark with ⋀ the possible places in the sentences where you could put the adverbs.

1 carefully (3 places)

Kelly carried the box from the car.

2 hard (1 place)

Lola practises to be a gymnast.

3 ferociously (2 places)

The lions growled at us.

4 easily (2 places)

The Italian team won the motorcycle rally.

5 skilfully (2 places)

He carved the piece of wood.

PRACTICE $\boxed{D}$ Underline the correct words in the brackets to complete the passage.

The men worked **1** (patient / patiently) under the hot sun. They **2** (skilful / skilfully) guided their water buffaloes up and down the open fields. The ploughs pulled by the buffaloes formed **3** (deep / deeply) furrows in the earth. Children followed **4** (happy / happily) behind their fathers, doing their share of the **5** (hard / hardly) work. They picked up sticks and stones and piled them **6** (careful / carefully) on one side. Soon they were tired and sat down **7** (quiet / quietly) to watch their fathers at work. A while later, some women entered the fields, their faces shaded from the **8** (fierce / fiercely) heat by large straw hats. Little bags of seeds hung **9** (loose / loosely) from their shoulders. Their fingers moved **10** (quick / quickly) as they scattered the rice seeds across the fields.

PRACTICE $\boxed{E}$ Tick the correct sentences.

1
  A He tried hard to score a goal.
  B He tried hardly to score a goal.

2
  A Tina answered correctly all the questions.
  B Tina answered all the questions correctly.

3
  A She washed the plates noisily.
  B She washed noisily the plates.

4
  A She sang sweetly at the concert.
  B Sweetly she sang at the concert.

5
  A The child smiled shy.
  B The child smiled shyly.

Fill in the blanks with the adverb forms of the words in the brackets.

The craftsmen of long ago worked (1) ___*painstakingly*___ (painstaking) at making furniture. Each piece was made (2) _____ (loving). Their wooden furniture had

(3) _____ (beautiful) carved doors, sides, tops and legs. Some pieces were

(4) _____ (rich) decorated with mother-of-pearl. Some craftsmen even made furniture without using any nails. They were able to fit the parts of furniture (5) _____ (perfect) after measuring and shaping pieces of wood (6) _____ (accurate).

Today, furniture is (7) _____ (usual) mass-produced. Factory workers have to work

(8) _____ (fast) to meet schedules. Supervisors ensure that the work is done

(9) _____ (good). The finished items are packed and sent (10) _____ (straight) to furniture shops.

Clearly, the modern method of making furniture is (11) _____ (complete) different from that of the old days.

YOUR SCORE

10

PRACTICE G Underline the mistakes in the sentences. Then write the correct words in the boxes.

1 I did everything slowly this morning and arrived lately at school, but was just in time for class.

2 The little girl threw the ball highly into the air, caught it expertly and passed it happily to her friend.

3 My brother won the competition and made us proudly of him.

4 The crowd watched breathlessly as the plane dived lowly and rose again immediately.

5 He acts good and sings beautifully. Many people admire him greatly.

YOUR SCORE

10

UNIT 7.1 SUBJECT-VERB AGREEMENT

positive statements

Look at the **A** and **B** sentences below. Find out why **B** is correct and **A** is wrong in the **Grammar Points** section.

GRAMMAR POINTS

1A	He at the office now.	✗	
1B	He **is** at the office now.	✓	1
2A	The postman **deliver** letters	✗	
2B	The postman **delivers** letters.	✓	2
3A	The water **are** cool.	✗	
3B	The water **is** cool.	✓	3
4A	Peter and Paul **cycles** to school.	✗	
4B	Peter and Paul **cycle** to school.	✓	4

GRAMMAR POINTS

1 Every sentence must have a subject and a verb. The subject can be a noun or a pronoun.

EXAMPLES:

Subject	Verb	
Rita noun	sings	English songs.
I pronoun	am	13 years old.

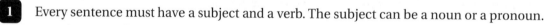

> **REMEMBER!**
> - The two basic types of verbs are main verbs and auxiliary verbs. The majority of verbs are main verbs. Auxiliary verbs are a small group of verbs including 'to be', 'to do', 'to have', **can**, **may**, etc. An auxiliary verb is also known as a 'helping verb'. It is used in combination with a main verb; it cannot stand on its own in a sentence.
>   EXAMPLE: He can speak as many as five languages.
>   (auxiliary verb) (main verb)
> - The verbs 'to be', 'to do' and 'to have' can be used as main verbs as well as auxiliary verbs.
>   EXAMPLES: My neighbours **have** four cars.   ('to have' as main verb)
>   I **have got** an idea!   ('to have' as auxiliary verb)

2 We use singular verbs for singular subjects and plural verbs for plural subjects.

EXAMPLES:

	Singular Subject	Plural Subject
the verb 'to be'	The boy **is** hungry. He **is** tired.	The boys **are** hungry. We **are** tired.
the verb 'like'	The monkey **likes** bananas. She **likes** chocolates.	The monkeys **like** bananas. They **like** chocolates.

54

Take note that the singular pronouns **I** and **you** are the only exceptions as they do not make use of singular verb forms.

EXAMPLES:

	Singular Subject	
the verb 'to be'	I **am** busy.	You **are** busy.
the verb 'like'	I **like** ice-cream.	You **like** ice-cream.

3 Uncountable nouns take singular verb forms.
EXAMPLE: The vinegar **is** in that bottle.

4 Two or more subjects joined by **and** always take a plural verb.
EXAMPLES: My father **and** my mother **work** in the city.
Alice **and** Janet **are** my neighbours.

PRACTICE A Complete the sentences in Column B by changing the verbs in Column A into their plural forms.

A	B
1 The cat sleeps on the floor.	The cats _sleep on the floor_____ .
2 A doctor takes care of patients.	Doctors _____ .
3 A bird has feathers.	Birds _____ .
4 The soldier is brave.	The soldiers _____ .
5 The child laughs happily.	The children _____ .
6 She plays netball very well.	They _____ .

YOUR SCORE 10

PRACTICE B In each sentence, the verb does not agree with the subject. Write the correct form of the verb in the box.

1 She already <u>know</u> the answer. | _knows_ |

2 Dad <u>wash</u> the car once a week.

3 The bus driver and the passengers <u>is</u> at the police station.

4 I <u>is</u> your friend.

5 Many tourists <u>enjoys</u> the food in France.

6 Anita <u>study</u> every night.

7 Gold <u>are</u> valuable.

8 They <u>gives</u> good service to the customers.

9 The sugar <u>are</u> in that cupboard.

10 He <u>save</u> a lot of money in the bank.

YOUR SCORE 10

11 The fishermen <u>goes</u> out to sea every day.

55

PRACTICE C Circle the verbs which can go with the subjects in the shaded boxes.

1 Jerry and Julie > are   does   have   takes

2 They > catches   do   has   prefer

3 A basket of flowers > is   have   makes   please

4 That tower > is   looks   need   rise

5 Many sheep > eats   follow   graze   has

YOUR SCORE
10

PRACTICE D Tick the correct boxes to complete the sentences.

1 The people ☐ was cheering / ☐ were cheering as the runners entered the stadium for the last lap of the marathon.

2 The new equipment ☐ are / ☐ is going to be used in the children's ward.

3 Vinegar and oil ☐ are / ☐ is blended to make a salad dressing.

4 The cattle ☐ are moving / ☐ is moving towards the valley.

5 These pieces of ancient pottery ☐ reveal / ☐ reveals to us the ceramic arts of ancient China.

6 Silver jewellery ☐ are / ☐ is popular nowadays.

7 The building of highways sometimes ☐ damage / ☐ damages the natural environment.

8 Joy on the faces of little children ☐ touch / ☐ touches the heart.

9 My parents ☐ prefer / ☐ prefers sailing to any other form of outdoor sport.

10 He ☐ has got / ☐ have got a lot of work to do before the opening of the exhibition.

YOUR SCORE
10

56

PRACTICE *E* Cross out the incorrect words in the boxes to complete the sentences.

1 We want to | take | takes | part in the concert.

2 The women's club | hold | holds | a meeting every fortnight.

3 Salt and pepper | are | is | important ingredients in cooking.

4 The president and the ministers | has | have | just entered the hall.

5 You | write | writes | very interesting short stories.

6 The people | was | were | silent when the judge spoke.

7 Hundreds of sheep | are grazing | is grazing | on the hillsides.

8 The water level in the river often | rise | rises | to a dangerous point.

9 Farmers in the Philippines | cultivate | cultivates | rice on terraced mountainsides.

10 The teenagers | are | is | busy pitching tents at the campsite.

YOUR SCORE
10

PRACTICE *F* Some verbs are missing from the passage below. Rewrite the passage and complete the sentences with some of the verbs in the box.

| carry | carries | has | have | is | are | put | puts | work | works |

Green Tea Grove a small town. It a large tea plantation. The cool climate here suitable for tea-growing. Many people in the town as tea pickers. They pick the young tea leaves and them in baskets. Then they these baskets of tea leaves to the factory for processing.

Green Tea Grove is a small town.

YOUR SCORE
10

57

UNIT 7.2 SUBJECT-VERB AGREEMENT

negative statements

Look at the **A** and **B** sentences below. Find out why **B** is correct and **A** is wrong in the **Grammar Points** section.

GRAMMAR POINTS

CHECKPOINT

1A	My parents **doesn't** like sugar in their coffee.	✗	
1B	My parents **don't** like sugar in their coffee.	✓	1
2A	The women **isn't** happy about this.	✗	
2B	The women **aren't** happy about this.	✓	2
3A	I **ain't** a small child anymore.	✗	
3B	I **am not** a small child anymore.	✓	3

GRAMMAR POINTS

1 We form the negative of most verbs by adding **doesn't** or **don't** before them.

(a) For a singular subject, we add **doesn't** and change the verb to its base form:
EXAMPLES: My brother **likes** sweets. → My brother **doesn't like** sweets.
She **washes** our clothes. → She **doesn't wash** our clothes.
He **has** many toys. → He **doesn't have** many toys.

(b) For a plural subject, and the singular pronouns **I** and **you**, we add **don't**:
EXAMPLES: My friends **like** sweets. → My friends **don't like** sweets.
You **sing** very well. → You **don't sing** very well.
I **have** many toys. → I **don't have** many toys.

Doesn't is the contracted form of **does not**, and **don't** is the contracted form of **do not**.

> ### REMEMBER!
> ■ A negative statement is a sentence which contains a word such as 'not', 'no', 'never' or 'nothing'.
> ■ The base form of a verb is the simplest form, without any letters added to the end. It is similar to the plural form of the verb in the present tense.
>
> | EXAMPLES: | base form | singular | past tense |
> |----|----|----|----|
> | | walk | walks | walked |
> | | brush | brushes | brushed |
> | | have | has | had |
> | | eat | eats | ate |

2 We form the negative of the verb 'to be' by changing it to **isn't** or **aren't**.

(a) For a singular subject, we change the verb to **isn't**:
EXAMPLES: Sam **is** here. → Sam **isn't** here.
It **is** raining. → It **isn't** raining.

(b) For a plural subject and the singular pronoun **you**, we change the verb to **aren't**:
   EXAMPLES: The children **are** here. → The children **aren't** here.
   You **are** my best friend. → You **aren't** my best friend.

Isn't is the contracted form of **is not** and **aren't** is the contracted form of **are not**.

3 For the singular pronoun **I**, we form the negative of the verb 'to be' like this:
   EXAMPLES: I **am** afraid of the dark. → I **am not** afraid of the dark.
   I **am** a member of the club. → I **am not** a member of the club.

Ain't should not be used as a contracted form of **am not**.

PRACTICE $\boxed{A}$ Complete the sentences with the negative forms of the underlined verbs.

1 He <u>owns</u> a piano.   She _does not/doesn't own a piano._

2 We <u>exercise</u> in the morning.   They _____

3 Mrs Fisher <u>is</u> at home.   Her sister _____

4 He <u>is</u> an artist.   We _____

5 My cat <u>has</u> a long tail.   My rabbit _____

6 They <u>have</u> blue eyes.   We _____

YOUR SCORE

10

PRACTICE $\boxed{B}$ Make sentences from the words in the boxes by using the negative forms of the verbs given.

1 Our neighbours | be | at home .

   Our neighbours are not/aren't at home.

2 Kim | want | an ice-cream .

   _____

3 Amy | own | a bicycle .

   _____

4 My cat | eat | mice .

   _____

5 She | be | the best actress in the movie .

   _____

6 We | be | in the school team .

   _____

YOUR SCORE

10

PRACTICE C Rearrange the words to form negative statements.

1 do — in — live — not — town — we.

_____

2 are — highway — houses — near — not — our — the.

_____

3 big — farm — is — not — our.

_____

4 a — cinema — does — not — have — the — village.

_____

5 area — do — in — many — not — our — see — tourists — we.

_____

YOUR SCORE

10

PRACTICE D Make sentences with the words given.

1

like	Jenny	✓
ice-cream	James	✗

Jenny likes ice-cream.
James does not/doesn't like ice-cream.

2

be	London	✓
a city	Japan	✗

London is a city.

_____

3

have	I	✓
an aquarium	Lily	✗

I have an aquarium.

_____

4

speak	My teacher	✓
Mandarin	My mother	✗

My teacher speaks Mandarin.

_____

5

be	oxygen	✓
gas	mercury	✗

Oxygen is a gas.

_____

6

have	a camel	✓
hump	a rhino	✗

A camel has a hump.

_____

YOUR SCORE

10

60

Underline the mistakes in negative verb forms in the sentences. Then write the correct words in the boxes.

1 I ain't coming today because I have no transport.

2 We don't wants to wait for Marie any longer.

3 She doesn't thinks her mother will let her come out with us.

4 Rosalind isn't fond of loud music. Her brother isn't share her views.

5 Our neighbours doesn't like to discuss their problems with us.

YOUR SCORE
10

PRACTICE F Underline the sentences that are wrong and rewrite them correctly.

Every day Laura makes sure she doesn't oversleep. She isn't want to be late for work. In the office she not waste time. She often works overtime. Laura's colleagues isn't as hardworking as she is. Most of them doesn't think she is doing the right thing. They feel she doesn't know how to enjoy life. Laura's parents also want her to slow down. They think it aren't wise of her to work such long hours. However, Laura isn't willing to change her ways.

1 _____

_____

2 _____

_____

3 _____

_____

4 _____

_____

5 _____

_____

YOUR SCORE
10

UNIT 7.3 SUBJECT-VERB AGREEMENT

positive questions

Look at the **A** and **B** sentences below. Find out why **B** is correct and **A** is wrong in the **Grammar Points** section.

			GRAMMAR POINTS
1A	**You are** thirsty?	✗	
1B	**Are you** thirsty?	✓	1
2A	**Is** the shops open today?	✗	
2B	**Are** the shops open today?	✓	2
3A	Does Mona **knows** the rules?	✗	
3B	Does Mona **know** the rules?	✓	3

GRAMMAR POINTS

1 Statements are sentences which give us information. Questions are sentences which ask the listener to give information. We normally do not make use of the statement form when asking for information. We use the question form.

EXAMPLES:

Statements	Questions
You are angry.	Are you angry?
You know him.	Do you know him?

2 We form questions with the verb 'to be' by placing the verb before the subject. Compare this to the statement form where the subject comes before the verb 'to be'.

EXAMPLES:

Statements	Questions
Subject + verb 'to be'	Verb 'to be' + subject
She **is** ill.	**Is** *she* ill?
The postman **is** late.	**Is** *the postman* late?
They **are** at home.	**Are** *they* at home?
Those girls **are** your students.	**Are** *those girls* your students?

Singular subjects take the verb **is**, except for the singular pronouns **I** and **you** which take **am** and **are** respectively. Plural subjects take the verb **are**.

3 We can form questions with most verbs by changing the verb to its base form, and adding the verb 'to do' before the subject.

(a) For a singular subject, we add the verb **does** before the subject:

EXAMPLES:

Statements	Questions
Subject + verb	**Does** + subject + base form of verb
Jenny **plays** hockey.	**Does** *Jenny* **play** hockey?
He **goes** to this school.	**Does** *he* **go** to this school?

(b) For a plural subject, and the singular pronouns **I** and **you**, we add the verb **do** before the subject.

EXAMPLES:

Statements	Questions
Subject + verb	**Do** + subject + base form of verb

The boys **play** hockey. **Do** *the boys* **play** hockey?
They **go** to this school. **Do** *they* **go** to this school?

PRACTICE *A* Change the following statements into questions.

1 You have a camera.

Do you have a camera?

2 She wears contact lenses.

3 Australia is near New Zealand.

4 Giant pandas eat bamboo leaves.

5 The campers are safe from wild animals.

6 Many tourists visit this cheesecake factory.

YOUR SCORE
10

PRACTICE *B* Underline the correct verbs.

A : Excuse me. **1** (Is / Are) you waiting for a taxi?

B : Yes. **2** (Do / Does) taxis come around here?

A : Not anymore. This place is almost deserted.

B : **3** (Is / Are) there any other way I can get to the train station?

A : **4** (Do / Does) you know Sam Mahone? He can drive you there.

B : **5** (Is / Are) he the one who runs the only store here?

A : Yes. **6** (Do / Does) you know where it is?

B : **7** (Is / Are) it the blue building down the road?

A : Yes. **8** (Do / Does) you want a lift? I'll take you there.

B : **9** (Is / Are) it all right with you?

A : Of course. **10** (Do / Does) you need help with the luggage?

B : No, thanks. I can manage.

YOUR SCORE
10

PRACTICE *C* Tick the correct verbs in the boxes.

1 ☐ Do / ☐ Does you ☐ want / ☐ wants to play with us?

2 ☐ Are / ☐ Is Andrea in the office today?

3 ☐ Does / ☐ Do Shane and James ☐ like / ☐ likes apple pie?

4 ☐ Are / ☐ Is all the teachers in the staffroom?

5 ☐ Does / ☐ Do they ☐ prefer / ☐ prefers orange juice or lemonade?

6 ☐ Are / ☐ Is your favourite games football and tennis?

7 ☐ Are / ☐ Is olive oil good for one's health?

YOUR SCORE

10

PRACTICE *D* Rearrange the words to form questions.

1 Does — drive — Derrick — work — to?
   Does Derrick drive to work?

2 a — dentist — Fiona — is?
   _____

3 clean — do — house — sons — the — their?
   _____

4 are — at — boys — gymnasium — the — the?
   _____

5 furniture — is — new — your?
   _____

6 daughters — does — fetch — his — Mr Hobbs — on — Wednesdays?
   _____

YOUR SCORE

10

64

PRACTICE *E* Underline the mistakes in verb forms in the sentences. Then write the correct words in the boxes.

1 Is my glasses in the drawer?

2 Does she spent all her time in the gym?

3 Does he wants to have lunch with us today?

4 Are the furniture ready for collection?

5 Do the choir members has their song sheets?

PRACTICE *F* Complete the questions by using the correct forms of the verb 'to be' or the verb 'to do'.

Tourist   : Good afternoon, officer. (1) _____ there a bank nearby?

Police officer : Yes, the Merchant Bank is just down the road.

Tourist   : Thank you. We also want to try some of the local food. (2) _____ you _____ (know) of any good restaurants here?

Police officer : Yes. (3) _____ you interested in Chinese food? There's a good restaurant around the corner.

Tourist   : (4) _____ it _____ (serve) very spicy food? We're not used to spicy food.

Police officer : Chinese food is quite mild.

Tourist   : (5) _____ the restaurant expensive?

Police officer : No, the prices are reasonable. (6) _____ you part of an organised tour group?

Tourist   : No, my wife and I are on our own.

Police officer : (7) _____ you _____ (have) any places of interest in mind?

Tourist   : Not really. (8) _____ bookshops here _____ (sell) maps?

Police officer : Some do. Instead of buying a map, try our Tourist Information Office.

Tourist   : (9) _____ it far from here?

Police officer : It's about 20 minutes away. (10) _____ you _____ (want) to go there? I'll show you the route.

Tourist   : That's very kind of you.

UNIT 8.1 PRESENT TENSE

simple and continuous

Look at the **A** and **B** sentences below. Find out why **B** is correct and **A** is wrong in the **Grammar Points** section.

GRAMMAR POINTS

				GRAMMAR POINTS
1A	Nita **is watering** the plants every morning.	✗		
1B	Nita **waters** the plants every morning.	✓		1a
2A	A square **is having** four sides.	✗		
2B	A square **has** four sides.	✓		1b
3A	The children **swim** now.	✗		
3B	The children **are swimming** now.	✓		2
4A	He **is do** his homework.	✗		
4B	He **is doing** his homework.	✓		3

GRAMMAR POINTS

Simple Present Tense

1 We use the simple present tense in these ways:

(a) to show habits and regular actions or to refer to current situations

> EXAMPLES: I **brush** my teeth every day. (habit)
> She **teaches** English every Saturday. (regular action)
> We **are** hungry. (current situation)

(b) to state general truths or facts

> EXAMPLES: The earth **is** round.   Birds **have** wings.

REMEMBER!

- The following are some words that are often used with verbs in the simple present tense to show habits or regular actions:

  > always   sometimes   usually   every day   every week   every year

- Verbs in the simple present tense are formed in these ways:

  For singular nouns and the pronouns **he/she/it**:

  (a) base form of verb + 's'
      EXAMPLE: take + s = takes
  (b) base form of verb + 'es'
      EXAMPLE: match + es = matches

  (c) base form of verb ending in 'y̶' 'i' + 'es'
      EXAMPLE: cry̶ i + es = cries

  For plural nouns and the pronouns **I/you/we/they**:

  base form of verb = present tense
  EXAMPLES: take, match, cry

Present Continuous Tense

2 We use the present continuous tense to show that an action is going on at the time of speaking or writing.

    EXAMPLES: **Simple Present Tense:**   I write letters every week. (regular action)
                  Present Continuous Tense: I am writing a letter now.

time taken to write

time when writing began   time when writing finished

NOW

> **REMEMBER!**
> - Words like **now** and **at the moment** often go with the present continuous tense.

3 We form the present continuous tense in this way:

    present tense form of the verb 'to be' + base form of verb + 'ing'

    EXAMPLES: I **am sewing** a dress.
                  Amanda **is cleaning** the floor.
                  They **are playing** outside.

PRACTICE *A*   Underline the correct forms of the verbs to complete the sentences.

1 The businessman (calls / is calling) for a taxi.

2 Mrs Thomas (teaches / is teaching) at the moment.

3 Lions and tigers (hunt / are hunting) for food.

4 We (read / are reading) the newspaper every day.

5 Sharon (buys / is buying) tickets for the movie now.

6 Anna and Ben (studying / are studying) in America.

7 I (wake up / waking up) at 6 a.m.

8 Sometimes Darren (cycles / is cycling) to school.

9 Mona usually (exercises / is exercising) in the morning.

10 Joy (is prepare / is preparing) lunch for us now.

YOUR SCORE
10

PRACTICE *B*   Fill in the blanks with the verbs in the boxes.

1 Mrs Kaplan _____ clothes every day.

   She _____ a dress now.

sews	is sewing

2 The postman _____ a letter to Aziz.

   He _____ letters every morning.

delivers	is delivering

3 Elephants _____ sugar cane.

   Dumbo the elephant _____ a juicy sugar cane now.

eat	is eating

4 My father and Uncle Paul _____ daily.

   They _____ round the park now.

jog	are jogging

5 Mr Lee _____ children to school in his bus in the morning.

   He _____ 20 children in his bus now.

takes
is taking

YOUR SCORE
10

67

PRACTICE _C_ Complete these sentences about Sarah by crossing out the wrong verb forms.

Sarah (1) | is | ~~are~~ | a policewoman. Her day (2) | begin | begins | early. She

(3) | is leaving | leaves | for work at 6 a.m. each day. She (4) | arrives | is arriving | at the police

station at 7.45 a.m. At 8 a.m. she and the other officers (5) | attend | attends | a meeting. Their police

chief Captain Costa (6) | talk | talks | to them about their duties for the day.

Sarah and her partner Bill usually (7) | patrol | patrols | a certain part of the city each day.

They (8) | are making | make | sure that the streets and back alleys (9) | is | are | safe for the public.

They visit shopping malls and video arcades to look for students who (10) | play | plays | truant.

Sarah's day usually (11) | end | ends | at 6.30 p.m.

YOUR SCORE
10

PRACTICE _D_ Complete the sentences with the present or present continuous tense of the verbs in the box.

| breathe | have | hurry | love | play |
| put | rest | snow | weave | write |

1 Maria, we _____ your cakes. They are delicious.

2 Darren _____ articles for a famous magazine.

3 Father _____ now. He is tired.

4 My little brother _____ home from school every afternoon to watch cartoons.

5 It _____ outside. Please put on your boots.

6 Dolphins _____ underwater through their blowholes.

7 Danny _____ tennis at the club every weekend.

8 We usually _____ recyclable things in special bins.

9 Dogs _____ a well-developed sense of smell.

10 The women _____ mats this afternoon.

YOUR SCORE
10

68

PRACTICE E Fill in the blanks with the simple present or present continuous tense form of the words in the box. Each word may only be used once.

| act | demonstrate | enjoy | help | leave | like |
| present | require | take | watch | work | |

Tess (1) _____works_____ as a cosmetics consultant in a large department store. Her job

(2) _____ her to be at her counter by 10.30 a.m. Before she (3) _____ her

house, Tess (4) _____ her mother with the washing.

Tess (5) _____ her work. She (6) _____ to teach people how to use

make-up. She is at her counter now. She (7) _____ the art of make-up to a group of

girls. One of them (8) _____ as her model. The other girls

(9) _____ closely as Tess expertly highlights the model's eyes. Tess

(10) _____ only a short while to apply powder and lipstick to the model's

face. Then she (11) _____ the stunning model to her audience.

YOUR SCORE
10

PRACTICE F Tick the correct boxes to complete the dialogue.

Paul : Where's Mum? I (1) [ ] has / [ ] have something exciting to tell her.

Penny : She (2) [ ] is watching / [ ] watches her favourite programme on TV so don't disturb her.

Paul : My friends (3) [ ] are waiting / [ ] wait for me outside and I am in a rush.

Penny : What is so exciting, anyway?

Paul : I (4) [ ] prefer / [ ] prefers to tell Mum myself.

Mum : Tell me what, dear?

Paul : Mum! I (5) [ ] want / [ ] wants you to be the first to know. I (6) [ ] am / [ ] is in the

state football team!

Mum : What! You (7) [ ] are playing / [ ] played in the state team now? That's wonderful.

You (8) [ ] follows / [ ] are following in your father's footsteps.

Paul : Our coach announced the names today. We (9) [ ] start / [ ] starting training right away.

He (10) [ ] insists / [ ] is insisting that we should get into shape fast. Our first game

YOUR SCORE
10

is only three months away.

69

UNIT 8.2 SIMPLE PAST TENSE

regular and irregular verbs

Look at the **A** and **B** sentences below. Find out why **B** is correct and **A** is wrong in the **Grammar Points** section.

CHECKPOINT

GRAMMAR POINTS

1A	I **save** 50 dollars last month.	✗	
1B	I **saved** 50 dollars last month.	✓	1
2A	Mrs Mason **teached** us this morning.	✗	
2B	Mrs Mason **taught** us this morning.	✓	2
3A	She **cutted** the vegetables just now.	✗	
3B	She **cut** the vegetables just now.	✓	3

GRAMMAR POINTS

1 We use the simple past tense to show that an action happened in the past.

EXAMPLES: I **worked** in Melbourne last year.
I **was** in Seoul in 1996.

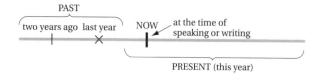

> **REMEMBER!**
> - The following are examples of some words that may be used with verbs in the past tense:
>
> | just now | yesterday |
> | last month | five years ago |

2 We add 'ed' to regular verbs to form the simple past tense. Irregular verbs take different forms.
EXAMPLES: I **cooked** spaghetti last night.   (regular verb – cook)
They **bought** a car last month.   (irregular verb – buy)

REMEMBER!
- The following are some ways of forming the past tense of regular verbs:
  - (a) base form of verb + 'ed'
    EXAMPLES: wash + ed = washed   show + ed = showed
  - (b) base form of verb ending in 'y' 'i' + 'ed'
    EXAMPLES: hurry i + ed = hurried   marry i + ed = married
  - (c) base form of verb ending in 'e' + 'ed'
    EXAMPLES: bathe + ed = bathed   advise + ed = advised   escape + ed = escaped

- Irregular verbs take different forms.
  EXAMPLES:

Base form	do	take	go	catch	choose	feel	draw	fight	lay	mean	ride	see	write
Past Tense	did	took	went	caught	chose	felt	drew	fought	laid	meant	rode	saw	wrote

---

The verb 'to be':

Pronouns	I	He/She/It	We/You/They
Present Tense	am	is	are
Past Tense	was	was	were

3 Some irregular verbs do not change to form the simple past tense. They keep the base form.
EXAMPLE: The ball **hit** him on the head just now.

REMEMBER!

Base form	beat	cost	cut	hit	hurt	let	put	set
Past Tense	beat	cost	cut	hit	hurt	let	put	set

PRACTICE *A* Complete the passage by crossing out the wrong verb forms.

I first (1) | ~~see~~ | saw | Rina the lioness on a safari in South Africa. I (2) | was | were | then in a
jeep with three other tourists and a guide. Rina (3) | laid | lay | quietly in the sun, unaware of our
presence. As we (4) | come | came | nearer, she (5) | stand | stood | up and (6) | stare | stared |
straight at us. I (7) | feel | felt | nervous but everyone else (8) | appear | appeared | calm.
The other tourists (9) | raise | raised | their cameras to film her. Suprisingly, Rina
(10) | stretch | stretched | lazily and (11) | seem | seemed | to pose for the cameras.

YOUR SCORE
10

PRACTICE *B* Change the verbs in bold in the paragraph to the past tense.

My brother and I (1) **are** at Uncle Ben's farm for a week. In the morning Aunt Dora (2) **fries** eggs
and (3) **makes** porridge for us. After breakfast we (4) **help** Uncle Ben. We (5) **collect** the hens' eggs. We
(6) **put** them in egg trays and (7) **leave** them in the kitchen. Then we (8) **feed** all the animals and
(9) **sweep** the farmyard. At about 10 a.m. we (10) **take** a rest under the trees. Then we (11) **clean** the
fish pond.

My brother and I (1) _____ *were* _____ at Uncle Ben's farm for a week. In the morning
Aunt Dora (2) _____ eggs and (3) _____ porridge for us. After breakfast we
(4) _____ Uncle Ben. We (5) _____ the hens' eggs. We (6) _____
them in egg trays and (7) _____ them in the kitchen. Then we (8) _____ all the
animals and (9) _____ the farmyard. At about 10 a.m. we (10) _____ a rest
under the trees. Then we (11) _____ the fish pond.

YOUR SCORE
10

PRACTICE C Fill in the blanks with the present tense or past tense form of the verbs in the brackets.

1 Lisa _____*painted*_____ her room yesterday. (paint)

2 I wash my clothes and _____ them in the morning. (dry)

3 The hungry baby _____ up at 4 a.m. this morning. (wake)

4 Last Saturday a thief _____ Lily's handbag from her car. (steal)

5 Riko _____ cakes for her family every week. (bake)

6 I _____ the racquets and Joan has the tennis balls. (have)

7 We _____ chess last weekend. (play)

8 They _____ in Europe two weeks ago. (be)

9 The pupils _____ at the factory an hour ago. (arrive)

10 She _____ her hand just now. (hurt)

11 He _____ his work for two hours every night. (revise)

PRACTICE D Complete the sentences with the correct verb forms of the words in the box.

| be | call | come | guess | hurry | lead |
| make | peep | prevent | remove | see | |

Rick (1) _____*was*_____ about to fall asleep when suddenly an unusual sound outside

(2) _____ him jump up. He (3) _____ from behind the curtains and

(4) _____ two men on a ladder. The ladder (5) _____ to the window of the

attic. Rick (6) _____ they were burglars. He quickly (7) _____ the police. Then

he (8) _____ upstairs and locked the door of the attic. After that he quietly stepped out of

the house and (9) _____ the ladder. In that way he (10) _____ the burglars from

escaping. The police (11) _____ soon after and took them away.

In each sentence, a mistake in verb form has been underlined. Write the correct form of the verb in the box.

1 Wendy <u>bathed</u> the baby now so she can't answer the phone.

2 We <u>find</u> our front door unlocked when we came home last Sunday.

3 The shoes <u>costs</u> too much so I can't afford them.

4 Our neighbours <u>bring</u> us a bag of tomatoes yesterday.

5 Scott <u>do</u> his work neatly and accurately.

6 Kevin <u>think</u> that we were not at home because nobody answered the doorbell.

7 Dad <u>letted</u> us stay up late yesterday because it is a holiday today.

8 Diana <u>burn</u> her hand when she tried to light the stove.

9 Aunt Celine <u>scold</u> me for spilling tea on her carpet.

10 These days we usually <u>went</u> out for dinner on Saturdays.

YOUR SCORE
10

PRACTICE F Fill in the blanks with the simple present or simple past tense form of the words in the brackets.

Judy (1) _____*goes*_____ (go) for a walk in the park at about 6 a.m. every morning. Her husband Ted usually (2) _____ (accompany) her but today he (3) _____ (remain) at home. He (4) _____ (have) a bad cold and needed to rest.

Judy (5) _____ (set) off by herself. Moments later, she (6) _____ (realise) that someone was following her. She (7) _____ (feel) extremely frightened. She quickly (8) _____ (head) for the main road where there were more people. Judy (9) _____ (run) all the way home. She (10) _____ (fling) open the door and shouted for Ted. He (11) _____ (come) running down the stairs to find out what was wrong.

YOUR SCORE
10

73

UNIT 8.3 PAST CONTINUOUS TENSE

Look at the **A** and **B** sentences below. Find out why **B** is correct and **A** is wrong in the **Grammar Points** section.

GRAMMAR POINTS

1A	This morning she **listening** to music in her room.	✗	
1B	This morning she **was listening** to music in her room.	✓	1
2A	At 5.30 p.m. yesterday he **is** driving home from work.	✗	
2B	At 5.30 p.m. yesterday he **was** driving home from work.	✓	2

GRAMMAR POINTS

1 We use the past continuous tense to show that an action was going on or being carried out in the past.

EXAMPLES:
At 6 p.m. yesterday I **was waiting** for a taxi outside the mall.
This afternoon Eric **was playing** tennis with Shane. Now he **is cleaning** his motorbike.

YESTERDAY		TODAY		TOMORROW
6 p.m.	4 p.m.	NOW		
I was waiting for a taxi.	Eric was playing tennis.	He is cleaning his motorbike.		

2 When we change from the present continuous tense to the past continuous tense, the verb 'to be' changes from the simple present tense to the simple past tense.

Pronouns	Present Continuous Tense simple present tense of the verb 'to be' + base form of verb + 'ing'	Past Continuous Tense simple past tense of the verb 'to be' + base form of verb + 'ing'
I	…am resting now.	…was resting just now.
He/She/It	…is sleeping now.	…was sleeping just now.
We/You/They	…are working now.	…were working just now.

74

PRACTICE $\boxed{A}$ Tick the sentences with the correct tenses.

1 Two months ago Rita won a prize for singing.

2 Last Tuesday we were swim at the lake.

3 Every morning Mum is waking me up to get ready for school.

4 Last night Ted was playing in the football finals at the stadium.

5 May usually goes home to visit her parents at weekends.

6 The maid is cooking dinner now. This afternoon she is ironing the clothes.

7 Please keep quiet. The baby is sleeping.

8 At sunset every day the fishing boats coming ashore.

9 Jack was bathing his dog just now.

10 Anna was attend a meeting at 9 a.m. today.

YOUR SCORE

10

PRACTICE $\boxed{B}$ Complete the sentences using the simple present, present continuous, simple past or past continuous tense form of the words in the brackets.

1 Coconut trees usually _____ (grow) along that coast.

2 He _____ (write) an article at this moment.

3 Please don't disturb me. I _____ (study) for my exams.

4 Dad _____ (repair) my bicycle all yesterday afternoon.

5 I _____ (talk) to Nina on the phone when the doorbell rang.

6 At 11 o'clock last night we _____ (enjoy) ourselves at a party.

7 We _____ (fall) sick after playing football in the rain yesterday.

8 The bookkeeper _____ (hurry) to the bank now.

9 The farmer usually _____ (feed) his animals early in the morning.

10 Look outside! The children _____ (climb) that tree!

YOUR SCORE

10

Tick the correct boxes to complete the sentences.

I (1) ☐ read / ☐ was reading a magazine at about 1 o'clock this afternoon when my best friend

Mandy (2) ☐ rushed / ☐ was rushing in. She (3) ☐ clutch / ☐ was clutching a page of the local newspaper

and her face (4) ☐ shines / ☐ shone with joy.

"We've won!" she cried. She (5) ☐ point / ☐ pointed to the paper but I did not understand.

I (6) ☐ stare / ☐ stared at her blankly. She (7) ☐ talked / ☐ was talking very fast and I (8) ☐ find / ☐ found
it hard to make out what she was saying.

"Do you remember the contest we both entered? We guessed the correct answers.
We've won $5000!"

I (9) ☐ leap / ☐ leapt up and (10) ☐ threw / ☐ throw my arms around her.

YOUR SCORE
10

PRACTICE D Fill in the blanks with the correct forms of the verbs in the box.

destroy	lend	make	prune	run
search	spray	spread	stand	tap

1 I _____ in the queue at the tax office for one hour yesterday.

2 Mum usually _____ me a mug of hot chocolate and toast before I drive
off to work.

3 Shirley _____ an advertising agency. She is the chief executive of the
firm.

4 Security forces _____ for the terrorist leader who bombed the police
station. They hope to arrest him soon.

5 Helen _____ the rose bushes in her garden at about 5 p.m. yesterday.

6 The viral infection _____ throughout the country last year.

7 A woodpecker _____ on our windowpane all night.

8 Sandra _____ me some money to pay for the books last week.

9 Dad _____ water on the car now to wash off the dust and dirt.

10 Last week, forest fires in the U.S. _____ thousands of acres
of valuable timber.

YOUR SCORE
10

76

Fill in the blanks with the simple past tense or past continuous tense of the verbs in the box.

be	crash	head	hear	notice	fall
shout	speed	swing	try	walk	

This is what happened. At about 7 a.m. yesterday we

(1) _____*were walking*_____ to school. We

(2) _____ the roar of an engine.

We turned round to see what it (3) _____ .

A white van (4) _____ down the main road.

The van driver (5) _____ to beat the traffic

lights.

At the same time, a motorcyclist in a side lane

(6) _____ towards the main road at great

speed. We saw him. The van driver didn't. We

(7) _____ to the motorcyclist to stop but he

didn't hear us.

The van driver suddenly (8) _____ the

motorcyclist. He (9) _____ to the right but it

was too late.

The van (10) _____ into a lamp post

on the other side of the road and the motorcycle

(11) _____ on its side.

YOUR SCORE

/10

UNIT 8.4 SIMPLE FUTURE TENSE

Look at the **A** and **B** sentences below. Find out why **B** is correct and **A** is wrong in the **Grammar Points** section.

CHECKPOINT

			GRAMMAR POINTS
1A	He **is** in Kuala Lumpur next Monday.	✗	
1B	He **will be** in Kuala Lumpur next Monday.	✓	1
2A	I **finish** the work later.	✗	
2B	I **will finish** the work later.	✓	2
3A	We **going to** travel to Tokyo this evening.	✗	
3B	We **are going to** travel to Tokyo this evening.	✓	3

GRAMMAR POINTS

1   We use the future tense to show future action.
EXAMPLES:
I **will go** to your place on Monday.
Mr Lopez **will call** us at 9 p.m. tomorrow.

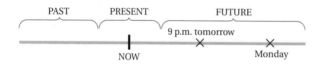

| PAST | PRESENT | FUTURE |

9 p.m. tomorrow

NOW   Monday

> **REMEMBER!**
> ■ The following are examples of some words that may be used with verbs in the future tense:
>
> | tomorrow | tomorrow night |
> | next Friday | next week |
> | next month | next year |

2   We form the simple future tense using **will** in this way:

   will + base form of verb

EXAMPLES:
Sue **will wash** the dishes later.
They **will visit** Mrs Law tomorrow evening.
The taxi **will be** here at 3 p.m.

> **REMEMBER!**
> ■ In the past, the simple future tense was formed using **shall** for **I** and **we**, and **will** for other pronouns and nouns.
>
> **EXAMPLES:**
> I **shall invite** Kay for dinner.
> We **shall go** to the supermarket on Tuesday.
>
> Nowadays, it is more common to use **will** for all nouns and pronouns.

3   We can also use the **going to** form for future action that is planned earlier or events that we think are likely to happen in the future. We form the simple future tense using **going to** in this way:

   present tense of the verb 'to be' + **going to** + base form of verb

EXAMPLES:
He **is going to play** golf on Saturday.
I **am going to swim** in the evening.
Oil prices **are going to rise** next week.

PRACTICE _A_   Cross out the incorrect verb forms to complete the passage.

The world (1) | will see | sees | great changes as the new century

(2) | progresses | progress | . As the Earth's population (3) | increases | increase | , people

(4) | need | will need | more houses, schools and hospitals. There (5) | will be | will | more mouths to

feed. Land which is already being farmed (6) | will produce | produce | too little to feed the

hungry billions.

In many countries today, people (7) | cutting | are cutting | down forests and clearing land for

settlements. These natural forests (8) | are | was | the homes of many species of wild animals. These

animals (9) | faced | are facing | extinction and (10) | will vanish | vanish | soon if man

does not take steps to protect them.

YOUR SCORE

10

PRACTICE _B_   Use the story about Steve to complete the story about James by changing the verbs in bold to the future tense.

Last year, Steve (1) **went** to school for the first time. The school bus (2) **picked** him up in the morning and his father (3) **fetched** him home in his car in the afternoon. In school, he (4) **listened** to his teacher carefully and (5) **did** all his work in class. He (6) **asked** his teacher some questions. At home, his elder brother (7) **helped** him with his homework.

Steve (8) **played** games in school with his friends. They (9) **did** many other things together. They (10) **were** happy. They (11) **helped** one another. They (12) **enjoyed** their time at school.

Begin your answer like this:

Next year, James will go to school for the first time. The school bus will pick him up in the morning

and _____

_____

_____

_____

_____

_____

_____

_____

_____

YOUR SCORE

10

PRACTICE $\boxed{C}$ In each sentence, a mistake in verb form has been underlined. Write the correct form of the verb in the box.

1 Ronald <u>was going</u> to participate in the motor-car rally next Saturday.

2 Linda <u>visit</u> her sister and her newborn nephew at the hospital tomorrow.

3 Prices of food and other necessities <u>is going</u> to rise as the festive season approaches.

4 Marion <u>will applied</u> for the post of a receptionist in that company tomorrow.

5 We <u>were hold</u> the meeting in two weeks' time.

6 My younger brother <u>are be</u> 16 years old at the end of this year.

7 The people in the coastal areas are going to <u>moved</u> to inland shelters as the typhoon prepares to strike.

8 The family <u>will taking</u> Mother out for a grand celebration on her birthday.

9 Becky's sister is going to <u>entering</u> college next year.

10 The senior students <u>were going</u> to organise a farewell dinner and dance next month.

PRACTICE $\boxed{D}$ Rearrange the words to form correct sentences.

1 exam — final — for — I — my — November — sit — this — will .

_____

2 be — football — in — next — our — Madrid — team — week — will .

_____

3 become — head — Linda — next — prefect — the — will — year .

_____

4 chocolate — Club — factory — Friday — next — our — Science — that — visit — will .

_____

5 going — his — house — is — my — neighbour — renovate — to .

_____

PRACTICE *E* Fill in the blanks with the correct forms of the verbs in the brackets.

Twenty-five years ago, my father (1) _____ (join) a well-known law firm as a junior lawyer. Dad was dedicated and smart and he (2) _____ (rise) quickly in the firm. Soon after, the firm (3) _____ (employ) Mum as the personal assistant to the manager. Dad and Mum fell in love and (4) _____ (get) married six months later.

Today, Dad (5) _____ (hold) the position of a senior partner in the firm. My parents raised three children. They (6) _____ (give) us plenty of love, encouragement and sound advice when we were young. We (7) _____ always _____ (be) grateful to them.

Next Friday, my parents (8) _____ (celebrate) their silver wedding anniversary — 25 years of happy marriage. My brothers and I (9) _____ (compere) an evening of entertainment. We (10) _____ (present) them with gifts to cherish as mementos.

YOUR SCORE

10

PRACTICE *F* Complete the interview with the simple past, present or future tense of the verbs in the brackets.

Rachel Khan : Miss Robson, how long will your stay in New Zealand last?

Julia Robson : I (1) _____ (be) here for three weeks — for the film 'The Restless Ones'.

Rachel Khan : I know Tom Hanson (2) _____ (fall) ill and could not continue to work as the director. Who (3) _____ (direct) the film now?

Julia Robson : Sam Wilson. He's in Australia at the moment. He (4) _____ (return) tomorrow.

Rachel Khan : What is your role in this film?

Julia Robson : I (5) _____ (be) the heroine, Sandra Wells.

Rachel Khan : Sandra Wells? Wasn't she an American writer who (6) _____ (spend) many years in Wellington in the late nineteenth century?

Julia Robson : Yes. The film is about her experiences.

Rachel Khan : That (7) _____ (sound) interesting.

Julia Robson : Interesting? It's almost like my life story. I myself (8) _____ (live) in Wellington when I was a little girl. My father (9) _____ (be) a diplomat then. I (10) _____ (have) a friend called Nancy. I wonder where she is now . . . .

YOUR SCORE

10

UNIT 8.5 FUTURE CONTINUOUS TENSE

Look at the **A** and **B** sentences below. Find out why **B** is correct and **A** is wrong in the **Grammar Points** section.

GRAMMAR POINTS

				GRAMMAR POINTS
1A	At 10 a.m. tomorrow they **attend** the meeting.		✗	
1B	At 10 a.m. tomorrow they **will be attending** the meeting.		✓	1
2A	I **will be play** squash with Chris tomorrow.		✗	
2B	I **will be playing** squash with Chris tomorrow.		✓	2

GRAMMAR POINTS

1 We use the future continuous tense to show that an action will be going on in the future.

EXAMPLES: At 11 p.m. tomorrow Janet **will be studying**.
He **will be waiting** for us at the bus stop after school.

YESTERDAY ~ 11 p.m.	NOW ~ 11 p.m.	TOMORROW ~ 11 p.m.
Janet was studying.	Janet is studying.	Janet will be studying.

2 We form the future continuous tense in this way:

will be + base form of verb + 'ing'

EXAMPLES: The teacher **will be visiting** his student this afternoon.
Al and I **will be travelling** to Mexico next week.

REMEMBER!

■ The future continuous tense can also be formed using **shall** for **I** and **we**, although it is more common to use **will** for all nouns and pronouns.

EXAMPLE: I **shall be singing** at the concert tomorrow night.

PRACTICE **A**   Tick the correct boxes to complete the sentences.

1 We ☐ arrived / ☐ will arrive at the park one hour from now.

2 Nicky ☐ is skating / ☐ will be skating now.

3 I ☐ hold / ☐ will be holding a barbecue tomorrow.

4 Jessie and her father ☐ are fishing / ☐ were fishing at the waterfalls now.

5 I ☐ take / ☐ will be taking my dog to the vet later.

6 In the evening, Olga usually ☐ listens / ☐ is listening to the news.

7 He ☐ sweeps / ☐ is sweeping the garden every day.

8 Alan and Nelson ☐ are swimming / ☐ will be swimming in the river at the moment.

9 Sally and Ben ☐ moved / ☐ will be moving house this weekend.

10 She ☐ found / ☐ finds a wallet on the road just now.

PRACTICE **B**   Fill in the blanks with the correct forms of the verbs in the brackets.

1 Grandpa will be _____ (leave) for China next Monday.

2 Trisha _____ (help) me find my book yesterday.

3 Dad _____ (mow) the lawn now.

4 We will be _____ (fly) to Canada tomorrow.

5 Marie _____ (borrow) three books from the library last week.

6 Mr Hunter _____ (take) his family for a holiday every year.

7 I _____ (clean) the kitchen now.

8 Thomas will be _____ (call) you next week.

9 Nurse Graham _____ (bathe) Mr Scott now.

10 They _____ (be) at the Science Museum tomorrow morning.

PRACTICE **C** Use the mind-map and the words in the box to make sentences in the future continuous tense.

1
Vicky — write the invitations and Carol — send them out

2
Sue — draw up the menu and then she — contact the caterers

6
Grandma — write a speech and Grandpa — deliver it

Things we'll be doing before Dad and Mum's 25th Wedding Anniversary

3
Kim — clean the house and Mel — decorate it

5
Tom — assemble the hi-fi system and Dad — test it

4
Dylan, Tom and I — put up the canopies and then we — arrange the tables and chairs

1 Vicky _____*will be writing*_____ the invitations and Carol _____*will be sending*_____ them out.

2 Sue _____ the menu and then she _____ the caterers.

3 Kim _____ the house and Mel _____ it.

4 Dylan, Tom and I _____ the canopies and then we _____ _____ the tables and chairs.

5 Tom _____ the hi-fi system and Dad _____ it.

6 Grandma _____ a speech and Grandpa _____ it.

YOUR SCORE
10

PRACTICE **D** Underline the correct verb forms in the dialogue.

Ben : The final term **1** (was ending / will be ending) next month. Our exams **2** (are / were) over and we have about three months to decide what we **3** (are going to do / were doing) next year.

David : I haven't made up my mind yet. My choice **4** (was / will be) Information Technology or Engineering. Dad **5** (hopes / hoped) that I will join his company after I finish my degree.

Ben : You **6** (are / were) so lucky. You already **7** (know / knew) what you want to do. I'm not sure where I **8** (was studying / will be studying) or which course I **9** (choose / will choose).

David : Ben, you **10** (are having / have) good management skills. You are able to organise things so well. I think you should study Business Management.

YOUR SCORE
10

Tick the correct boxes to complete the sentences.

Next Saturday I (1) ☐ going to celebrate / ☐ will be celebrating my twenty-first birthday. I (2) ☐ enjoy / ☐ will enjoy

the legal status of an adult. My parents (3) ☐ going to buy / ☐ will be buying me a car as a present. It is a

second-hand Honda Civic but I don't mind. To me it (4) ☐ meant / ☐ will mean independence and time

saved. I (5) ☐ was / ☐ will be free to go wherever I want to and I don't have to wait for buses or taxis.

Dad (6) ☐ gives / ☐ will be giving me the keys just before my birthday. My friends (7) ☐ are / ☐ is

thrilled. I (8) ☐ am going to drives / ☐ will be driving to college next week and I (9) ☐ promised / ☐ will promise to

give them a lift. My life (10) ☐ definitely changed / ☐ will definitely change after my birthday.

YOUR SCORE
10

PRACTICE **F** Fill in the blanks with the correct verbs in the brackets.

Cindy Jacobs (1) _____ (live / lives) in Mexico City.

She (2) _____ (joined / is joining) a large advertising agency two years ago

as a junior executive. Cindy (3) _____ (learnt / was learning) her job well

and today she (4) _____ (is / will be) a senior executive.

Cindy's company has several plans for her. In February, it (5) _____

(sends / will be sending) her to New York for further training. She (6) _____

(attended / will be attending) a course in management there. When she (7) _____

(is returning / returns) home, the company (8) _____ (make / will make)

her the sales manager.

Next week, Cindy (9) _____ (went / will be going) to

Victoria City to spend some time with her parents. She (10) _____

(plans / will plan) to see her old friends too before leaving.

YOUR SCORE
10

UNIT 9 SUBJECT AND PREDICATE

Look at the **A** and **B** sentences below. Find out why **B** is correct and **A** is wrong in the **Grammar Points** section.

 **CHECKPOINT**

1A	Can sit here.	✗	
1B	**We** can sit here.	✓	1
2A	Very cute **she is**.	✗	
2B	**She is** very cute.	✓	2
3A	The window open.	✗	
3B	The window **is** open.	✓	3
4A	She **answered well** the question.	✗	
4B	She **answered** the question **well**.	✓	4

GRAMMAR POINTS

1 A sentence usually has a **subject** (what the sentence is about) and a **predicate** (the part of the sentence which gives information about the subject).

EXAMPLES:

SUBJECT	PREDICATE
Fish	swim.
Cairo	is the capital of Egypt.
My cousin	likes to eat ice-cream and popcorn.

2 The **subject** usually comes before the predicate.

EXAMPLE: **You** are very clever. ✓ Very clever you are. ✗

3 The predicate must contain at least one **verb**.

EXAMPLE: The trees **are** green. ✓ The trees green. ✗

4 The predicate may also contain an object, a complement or an adverbial. The object or complement comes immediately after the verb.

EXAMPLES:

SUBJECT (what the sentence is about)	VERB	OBJECT (what my cat drinks)
My cat	drinks	chocolate milk.

SUBJECT (what the sentence is about)	VERB	COMPLEMENT (what Mrs Lodge is)
Mrs Lodge	is	an architect.

The adverbial often appears at the end of the sentence: after the verb, object or complement.

EXAMPLES:

SUBJECT	VERB	ADVERBIAL
She	slept	on the bus.

SUBJECT	VERB	OBJECT	ADVERBIAL
My neighbour	washes	his car	every Sunday.

SUBJECT	VERB	COMPLEMENT	ADVERBIAL
He	was	my teacher	last year.

REMEMBER!

- The object is the person or thing that the subject does something to.
- A complement often describes a quality or characteristic of the subject or object.
  EXAMPLE: He is *a kind boy.*
- A complement can also tell us the identity of the subject or object.
  EXAMPLE: She is *my mother.*
- An adverbial tells us more about an action, event or state mentioned in the sentence.
  EXAMPLES: • when it happened (We watched a movie *yesterday.*)
  • where it happened (They played volleyball *at the beach.*)
  • how it happened (The old lady climbed the stairs *slowly and carefully.*)

PRACTICE *A* Some of the sentences do not have verbs. Mark with ⋀ wherever a verb is missing.

1 Snakes⋀dangerous animals.

2 I do yoga twice a week.

3 Tokyo a large city.

4 We celebrate Christmas in December.

5 I from the United States.

6 You pretty in that dress.

7 Mum made a tuna sandwich for me.

8 Dad works for a telephone company.

9 Paul at the station on time.

10 Larry here just now.

11 Carol dived into the swimming pool.

YOUR SCORE
10

PRACTICE *B* Rearrange the words to form correct sentences.

1 a — at — bought — the — supermarket — watermelons — we.

_____

2 friendly — is — neighbour — our.

_____

3 food — likes — Hans — spicy.

_____

4 fast — finished — her — she — work.

_____

5 he — manager — the — there — was.

YOUR SCORE
10

_____

87

1 She sweeps the floor every morning. (   )
2 They caught the robber. (   )
3 Susan plays beautifully the piano. (   )
4 His car hit the lamppost. (   )
5 The balloons are floating. (   )
6 Cannot park here. (   )
7 My pet is a squirrel. (   )
8 I saw there some seagulls. (   )
9 That man Mr Fynch. (   )
10 She is in Asia famous. (   )

YOUR SCORE
10

PRACTICE $\boxed{D}$ Correct the following sentences using suitable words in the box.

| are | has | have | is | makes |
| manager | porridge | you | was | |

1 Those plants unusual.
   Those plants are unusual.

2 Chris is a good.
   _____

3 Some camels two humps.
   _____

4 Can phone your mother now.
   _____

5 The weather fine yesterday.
   _____

6 My neighbour makes for breakfast.
   _____

YOUR SCORE
10

PRACTICE E Circle the letters of the sentences that are correct.

1   **A**   The taxi driver's children very lively.
    (B)   The taxi driver's children are very lively.
    C   Very lively the taxi driver's children.

2   **A**   The western sky is beautiful at sunset.
    B   At sunset the western sky is beautiful.
    C   The western sky looks beautiful at sunset.

3   **A**   In her backyard she planted vegetables.
    B   She planted in her backyard vegetables.
    C   She planted vegetables in her backyard.

4   **A**   Didn't see you at the school fair.
    B   I didn't see you at the school fair.
    C   We didn't see you at the school fair.

5   **A**   Lovingly the girl stroked the horse's head.
    B   The girl stroked the horse's head lovingly.
    C   The girl stroked lovingly the horse's head.

6   **A**   Suits him very well the army uniform.
    B   The army uniform suits very well him.
    C   The army uniform suits him very well.

YOUR SCORE
10

PRACTICE F Underline the sentences in the passage that are incorrect. Rewrite the sentences correctly.

Ian a very quiet boy. Not many people know about his talent. He draws in his room at night excellent cartoons.

During the day he watches and listens to people around him. Their funny behaviour and words he notices. At night he turns them into cartoons. Makes them even funnier than they are.

Once Ian showed a teacher his drawings of her in a cartoon series. She laughed heartily. She said, "You a lot of talent." Later she said, "You like and understand people. That's why your cartoons are wonderful." The teacher is sure that Ian will be in his country one of the best cartoonists.

1   *Ian is a very quiet boy.* _____

2   _____

3   _____

4   _____

5   _____

6   _____

YOUR SCORE
10

UNIT 10 FINITE AND NON-FINITE VERBS

Look at the **A** and **B** sentences below. Find out why **B** is correct and **A** is wrong in the **Grammar Points** section.

GRAMMAR POINTS

1A	The dolphin **swimming**.	✗	
1B	The dolphin **is swimming**.	✓	1
2A	Everybody **to sing** a song.	✗	
2B	Everybody **has to sing** a song.	✓	2

GRAMMAR POINTS

1 A verb ending in 'ing' is a non-finite verb. It cannot exist on its own. We usually add the verb 'to be' before it to turn it into a finite verb and make the sentence complete.

EXAMPLE: **Non-Finite Verb** **Finite Verb**

The baby **crying**. ✗   The baby **is crying**. ✓

2 A verb with **to** before it is also a non-finite verb. It, too, cannot exist on its own. We usually add a finite verb before the non-finite verb to make the sentence complete.

EXAMPLES: **Non-Finite Verbs** **Finite Verbs**

All of them **to leave** now. ✗   All of them **are to leave** now. ✓

Everyone **to wear** a uniform. ✗   Everyone **has to wear** a uniform. ✓

REMEMBER!

■ A sentence must have at least one finite verb.

■ A finite verb changes its form according to the tense and subject of the sentence. The finite verbs have been highlighted in these examples:

Present tense	:	Today he **wants** to go to the park.
Past tense	:	Yesterday he **wanted** to go to the park.
Future tense	:	Tomorrow he **will want** to go to the park.
Singular subject	:	She **wants** to go to the park.
Plural subject	:	They **want** to go to the park.

Notice that the verb 'to go' which is a non-finite verb remains the same in all the sentences.

PRACTICE $\boxed{A}$ Underline the finite verbs in the sentences.

1 These shoes <u>cost</u> a lot.

2 We heard the children singing funny songs.

3 Julia had to learn dancing for her part in the movie.

4 Reading and drawing are my favourite activities.

5 You have to finish cleaning the house by noon.

6 Our hostess did everything to make us comfortable.

7 I am waiting for them to apologise to me.

8 Touring South America was a fascinating experience.

9 We are to be at the airport by 10 a.m.

10 Rachel is trying hard to improve her English.

11 I am to report for duty on Monday.

PRACTICE $\boxed{B}$ Tick the sentences that are correct.

1 ☐ A They to come yesterday but they could not.
  ☐ B They were to come yesterday but they could not.

2 ☐ A That ship is sailing to Alaska.
  ☐ B That ship sailing to Alaska.

3 ☐ A I have to rush to the hospital now.
  ☐ B I to rush to the hospital now.

4 ☐ A She to finish the report last night.
  ☐ B She had to finish the report last night.

5 ☐ A I am drawing your face now.
  ☐ B I drawing your face now.

91

Complete the sentences with the correct words in the brackets.

The brakes on my bicycle (1) _____ (was / were) not reliable. "You(2) _____ (have to repair / to repair) them," said my father but I (3) _____ (am / was) always too busy to go to the workshop. Each day I continued (4) _____ (cycled / to cycle) to school and back.

Then, late one evening, my brakes (5) _____ (failed / failing)! I nearly (6) _____ (knocking / knocked) an old lady down. I said to myself, "I (7) _____ (taking care / will take care) of my bicycle from now on."

Today I am still (8) _____ (ride / riding) my dear old bicycle. All its parts are good. When any part (9) _____ (gives / giving) trouble, I (10) _____ (repair / to repair) it immediately.

YOUR SCORE

/ 10

PRACTICE $\boxed{D}$ Rewrite the sentences correctly by turning the non-finite verbs into finite verbs. Use the words in the boxes to help you.

1 The students to go to the stadium now. $\boxed{\text{are}}$

_____

2 The factory workers to be ready for a fire drill. $\boxed{\text{have}}$

_____

3 The goose chasing the thief. $\boxed{\text{is}}$

_____

4 Susie to learn Japanese next year. $\boxed{\text{wants}}$

_____

5 Our music teacher training the choir for our concert. $\boxed{\text{is}}$

_____

YOUR SCORE

/ 10

PRACTICE E Underline the mistakes in verb forms in the sentences. Then write the correct words in the boxes.

1 The moon shining brightly that night. The coconut palms were swaying. The beach looked
wonderful and I wanted to stay there forever.

was shining

2 Careless people often meet with accidents. You to be careful all the time. Concentrate when you
are crossing the road.

3 Kim had only two minutes left. She had to be at the helicopter pad at 5 a.m. sharp. She running
very fast because the helicopter would not wait long for her.

4 Every year we try to visit a different place. Last year we decide to go to Egypt and next year we are
going to see our friends in Spain.

5 I have to do a lot of work nowadays and I have very little time for relaxation. A few years ago I
seemed to have more time. Maybe I not dividing my time well now.

6 All soldiers to report to their sergeants at once. This is an emergency. We must evacuate the
campsite as soon as possible.

YOUR SCORE

10

PRACTICE F Complete the poem with the correct words in the box.

am	is	bring	flow	had	love	make	play
are	were	brought	flowed	have	loved	making	played

Grandpa : Long ago, dear little boy,

This place (1) _____*brought*_____ me a lot of joy.

The river (2) _____ clear and clean

Through the forest thick and green.

I (3) _____ the fresh air and cool breeze.

I (4) _____ all day among the trees.

Child : Oh Grandpa, you (5) _____ me sad

Because I don't (6) _____ what you (7) _____ .

Now the river (8) _____ dirty and slow.

Soon it will not want to (9) _____ .

I (10) _____ breathing polluted air.

Oh Grandpa, it isn't fair!

They (11) _____ chopping down the trees.

Will you tell them to stop, please?

YOUR SCORE

10

93

UNIT 11 QUESTION TAGS

isn't and aren't

Look at the **A** and **B** sentences below. Find out why **B** is correct and **A** is wrong in the **Grammar Points** section.

			GRAMMAR POINTS
1A	This is an orchid, **is it**?	✗	
1B	This is an orchid, **isn't it**?	✓	1a
2A	He is your friend, **is not he**?	✗	
2B	He is your friend, **isn't he**?	✓	1b
3A	James is an architect, **isn't James**?	✗	
3B	James is an architect, **isn't he**?	✓	1c
4A	You are Fay's brother, **isn't it**?	✗	
4B	You are Fay's brother, **aren't you**?	✓	2

GRAMMAR POINTS

1 When writing question tags, we usually follow these rules:

(a) use negative question tags with positive statements; the verb 'to be' in the question tag must be the negative form of the verb 'to be' in the statement

   EXAMPLES: It **is** raining, **isn't** it?
   They **are** your classmates, **aren't** they?

(b) use short forms

   EXAMPLE: use **aren't** instead of **are not**:
   Those shoes are new, **aren't** they?

(c) use pronouns, not nouns or noun phrases

   EXAMPLE:

   Sheila is John's sister, isn't **she**? ✓

   Sheila is John's sister, isn't **Sheila**? ✗

> **REMEMBER!**
> - A statement can be turned into a question by adding a question tag at the end of it.
>   **EXAMPLE:**
>   This book is very interesting , isn't it?
>   _____
>   (statement) (question tag)
>
> - A question tag is used to
>   (a) check whether something is true
>   **EXAMPLE:**
>   Your brother is a lawyer, **isn't he**?
>
>   (b) find out if someone agrees with us
>   **EXAMPLE:**
>   This dress is beautiful, **isn't it**?
>
> - There is no short form for **am not** so **aren't** is used to form question tags instead.
>   **EXAMPLE:** I **am** in the team, **aren't** I?

2 The pronoun in a question tag must agree with the subject of the statement.

   EXAMPLE:

   (Your uncle) is a good singer, isn't (he)? ✓   (Your uncle) is a good singer, isn't (it)? ✗

PRACTICE **A** Fill in the blanks with question tags. Use the words in Box One and Box Two to form the question tags. Each word may be used more than once.

aren't	isn't		he	I	it	she	they	we	you
Box One						**Box Two**			

1 Your mother is a teacher, _____ ?

2 Roses are beautiful, _____ ?

3 That building is a temple, _____ ?

4 We are doing well, _____ ?

5 I am a fast runner, _____ ?

6 The deer and the giraffe are docile animals, _____ ?

7 You and I are taking the same bus, _____ ?

8 This little boy is clever, _____ ?

9 You are a footballer, _____ ?

10 That monkey is very playful, _____ ?

YOUR SCORE
10

PRACTICE **B** Add a question tag at the end of each statement.

1 This hockey stick is hers, _____ ?

2 I am in the football team, _____ ?

3 Ro and Jo are twins, _____ ?

4 You, Rose and I are good friends, _____ ?

5 The meal is delicious, _____ ?

6 That policewoman is helpful, _____ ?

7 You are angry with him, _____ ?

8 Mr Hill is your uncle, _____ ?

9 Lizards are reptiles, _____ ?

10 It is hot today, _____ ?

YOUR SCORE
10

PRACTICE *C*   Match Column A with Column B by writing the correct numbers in the boxes.

Column A

1	Billy is Tom's younger brother,
2	Those houses are as big as these,
3	Susan is angry with us,
4	You are coming for the concert,
5	That pink dress is beautiful,
6	We are tall and strong,

Column B

[ ]	aren't you?
[ ]	aren't we?
[ ]	isn't it?
[ ]	isn't she?
[ ]	aren't they?
1	isn't he?

YOUR SCORE

10

PRACTICE *D*   Complete the dialogue with suitable question tags.

Bobby :   Mum, it's raining hard, (1) _____ ?

Mum :   Yes, dear.

Bobby :   The plants are getting wet, (2) _____ ?

Mum :   Yes, but they need the rain.

Bobby :   Mum, Tracy is coming back from school, (3) _____ ?

Mum :   Yes, dear. You are waiting for her, (4) _____ ?

Bobby :   Yes. I want her to play with me.

Mum :   Ben and Jake are too busy to play with you, (5) _____ ?

Bobby :   They say I'm too small. I'm going to grow tall like them, (6) _____ ?

Mum :   Of course you are!

Bobby :   Mum, why isn't Tracy here? It's time for her to come home, (7) _____ ?

Mum :   Yes. Look! It's her bus, (8) _____ ?

Bobby :   Quick, Tracy! Come in.

Mum :   Here's a towel. You are cold, (9) _____ ?

Bobby :   Have a hot drink.

Tracy :   Thanks.

Bobby :   I'm a good brother, (10) _____ ?

Tracy :   Yes, you are.

YOUR SCORE

10

PRACTICE $\boxed{E}$ Circle the letters of the sentences that use question tags correctly.

1 Ⓐ One of your sisters is a strong swimmer, isn't she?
  Ⓑ Your sister Lydia is a strong swimmer, isn't she?
  C Lydia is a strong swimmer, isn't Lydia?

2 A This market is noisy, is it?
  B This market is noisy, isn't it?
  C Most markets are noisy, aren't they?

3 A Your husband is an animal lover like you, aren't you?
  B Your husband is an animal lover like you, isn't he?
  C You and your husband are animal lovers, aren't you?

4 A I am skating quite well, aren't I?
  B I am skating quite well, am not I?
  C You and I are skating quite well, aren't we?

5 A Those cattle are grazing on your land, aren't they?
  B That cow is grazing on your land, isn't it?
  C Those cattle is grazing on your land, isn't it?

6 A You and the Shaws are now members of the same club, aren't you?
  B You and the Shaws are now members of the same club, aren't they?
  C The Shaws are now members of your club, aren't they?

YOUR SCORE
10

PRACTICE $\boxed{F}$ Some of the sentences use correct question tags and some use incorrect ones. Underline the incorrect question tags and write the correct words in the boxes.

1 You are the new typist, <u>isn't it?</u>	*aren't you?*
2 The waves are getting rough, aren't they?	
3 I am a little too plump, am I?	
4 She is your sister's housemate, aren't they?	
5 You and I are going to share this computer, aren't we?	
6 Your Dad is as funny as mine, aren't they?	
7 The sea breeze is pleasant, isn't it?	
8 The largest of the mangoes is ripe, aren't they?	
9 We are both bookworms, are not we?	
10 You and Sally are flying off tonight, aren't you?	
11 It's cool in the mountains, isn't it?	

YOUR SCORE
10

UNIT 12.1 WH-QUESTIONS

Look at the **A** and **B** sentences below. Find out why **B** is correct and **A** is wrong in the **Grammar Points** section.

CHECKPOINT

			GRAMMAR POINTS
1A	You want to see **what**?	✗	
1B	**What** do you want to see?	✓	1
2A	**Where your** neighbours?	✗	
2B	**Where are your** neighbours?	✓	2
3A	When did they **went** to Spain?	✗	
3B	When did they **go** to Spain?	✓	3

GRAMMAR POINTS

1 We always begin a wh-question with a wh-word. The wh-words are as follows:

| Who | Whom | Whose | What | Which | Where | When | Why | How |

EXAMPLE:

Why were you absent yesterday? ✓

Yesterday why you were absent? ✗

> **REMEMBER!**
> - Wh-words are also known as interrogative words or questions words. They are words used in the asking of questions and they are called wh-words as most of them begin with 'wh'.
>   **EXAMPLES:** What is your name?
>   Whose bag is this?
> - During conversation, a wh-word alone can be used as a question. However, this is not acceptable in writing.
>   **EXAMPLE:** In conversation:
>   A: Someone here ordered a pizza.
>   B: Who?
>   In writing:
>   Who ordered a pizza?

2 Every wh-question must have a finite verb to make it complete.

EXAMPLES: When **is** the concert? ✓

When the concert? ✗

What **are** you doing? ✓

What you **doing**? ✗

3 When we use the verb 'to do' in wh-questions, the main verb in the question has to be in its base form.

EXAMPLES: Where does she **live**? ✓   Why did Pat **telephone** you? ✓

Where does she **lives**? ✗   Why did Pat **telephones** you? ✗

Where does she **living**? ✗   Why did Pat **telephoned** you? ✗

PRACTICE $\boxed{A}$ Tick the questions that are correct.

1   You will come when?

2   How much is this shirt?

3   When does he leave for Egypt?

4   Whose this wallet?

5   This dress is how much?

6   Which is yours?

7   Who did you met at Mark's house?

8   Why Dad laughing?

9   What did the policeman say?

10   Where are my football boots?

YOUR SCORE /10

PRACTICE $\boxed{B}$ Complete the questions with the correct words in the boxes.

1   _____ this morning?

| Where was he |
| He was where |

2   _____ apple pie?

| How do you make |
| How did you made |

3   _____ at the police station yesterday?

| Why were you |
| Why are you |

4   _____ to see the movie?

| When do they want |
| When do they wanting |

5   _____ the neatest handwriting?

| Which student has |
| Which student having |

PRACTICE $\boxed{C}$ Circle the letters of the questions that are correct.

1   Ⓐ   Where is Nepal?   B   Nepal is where?

2   A   Where does your mother works?   B   Where does your mother work?

3   A   When Jill coming?   B   When is Jill coming?

4   A   Why did they talk to you?   B   Why did they talked to you?

5   A   These drawings are whose?   B   Whose are these drawings?

6   A   How old are these maps?   B   How old these maps?

YOUR SCORE /10

YOUR SCORE /10

PRACTICE **D** Tick the correct boxes to complete the questions.

1 Why [ ] did / doing you [ ] leave / left the school in a hurry?

2 Where [ ] are you / you [ ] hang / hanging those balloons?

3 When [ ] do / doing Henry and Ken [ ] finishes / finish their exam?

4 How [ ] does Jenny / Jenny does [ ] made / make these dolls?

5 [ ] When are your cousins / Your cousins when are [ ] return / returning to Argentina?

PRACTICE **E** In each question, the finite verb in the box is missing. It should be at one of the two places marked ⋀ . Circle the correct ⋀ .

1 ⋀ Who ⋀ in the meeting room?   is

2 What ⋀ the matter ⋀ with Hannah?   is

3 Why ⋀ Kathy and Jim ⋀ so upset last night?   were

4 Which ⋀ college ⋀ your brothers in?   are

5 ⋀ When ⋀ Sports Day last year?   was

6 How far ⋀ Kyoto ⋀ from Tokyo?   is

7 How much pepper ⋀ there ⋀ in this packet?   is

8 Whose ⋀ design ⋀ the most colourful?   was

9 Where ⋀ my earrings ⋀ ?   are

10 How many ⋀ students ⋀ absent yesterday?   were

PRACTICE F Rewrite the questions and add in the verbs given in brackets.

1 Why you sad? (are)
   Why are you sad?
   _____

2 Which Edward's parcel? (is)
   _____

3 Who she talking to just now? (was)
   _____

4 When you appear on television? (do)
   _____

5 What those restaurants serve for breakfast? (do)
   _____

6 How many members the Drama Society have? (does)
   _____

PRACTICE G Rewrite the questions and correct the mistakes.

1 What Paige's ambition is?
   What is Paige's ambition?
   _____

2 Which book Robert does want?
   _____

3 Is who in charge of this games stall?
   _____

4 When you taking the driving test?
   _____

5 Whose house did the thieves breaking into?
   _____

6 Why the workers running out of the factory?
   _____

UNIT 12.2 WH-QUESTIONS

who

Look at the **A** and **B** sentences below. Find out why **B** is correct and **A** is wrong in the **Grammar Points** section.

			GRAMMAR POINTS
1A	Who **is** those men in black suits?	✗	
1B	Who **are** those men in black suits?	✓	1
2A	Who **want** a drink?	✗	
2B	Who **wants** a drink?	✓	2
3A	Who **is likes** football?	✗	
3B	Who **likes** football?	✓	3
4A	Who **knocking** on the door?	✗	
4B	Who **is knocking** on the door?	✓	4

GRAMMAR POINTS

1 In a **Who** question, the verb 'to be' must agree in tense and number with the noun it points to.

EXAMPLES:

Present tense

singular

Who **is** your **teacher**? (= your teacher this year)

plural

Who **are** your **team-mates**? (= your team-mates today)

Past tense

singular

Who **was** that **singer**? (= that singer at last night's concert)

plural

Who **were** the **speakers**? (= the speakers at yesterday's talk)

2 We usually use the **singular** form of a **main verb** with a **Who** question that is in the **present tense**.

EXAMPLES: Who **likes** chess? ✓

Who **like** chess? ✗

Who **knows** the answer? ✓

Who **know** the answer? ✗

REMEMBER!

- **Who** is used to ask questions about people's identity.

EXAMPLES:
Who are you?
(I am Jason.)

Who broke Mother's vase?
(Little Billy broke it.)

Who gave you this story book?
(My aunt gave me this story book.)

- Traditionally, **who** is used as the subject of the verb in a question, and **whom** is used as the object of the verb.

EXAMPLE:

subject   object
Question: Who called Alice ?

object   subject
Question: Whom did James call?

subject   object
Answer: James called Alice .

However, nowadays, it is more common to use **who** as both the subject and object of the verb.

102

3   We do not use the verb 'to be' together with a singular or plural main verb.

     EXAMPLE: Who **lives** next door to you?   ☑

                   Who **is** next door to you?   ☑

                   Who **is lives** next door to you?   ✗

4   We must use the verb 'to be' together with the 'ing' form of the main verb in a **Who** question.

     EXAMPLES: Finite Verbs   Non-finite Verbs

            Who **is playing** the piano now?   ☑   Who **playing** the piano now?   ✗

            Who **was shouting** just now?   ☑   Who **shouting** just now?   ✗

PRACTICE *A*   Tick the questions that are correct.

1   Who were at Nina's party last night?

2   Who coming tomorrow?

3   Who is talk loudly?

4   Who has my suitcase?

5   Who attended the meeting yesterday?

6   Who those children over there?

7   Who scored the highest marks for English?

8   Who at the airport this morning?

9   Who was your opponent in the tennis finals?

10   Who play hockey?

YOUR SCORE

10

PRACTICE *B*   Rearrange the words to form questions.

1   Italian — speaks — who?

    Who speaks Italian?

2   flowers — sent — these — who?

3   are — people — those — who?

4   a — baking — cake — is — who?

5   goalkeeper — the — was — who?

6   a — glass — of — wants — water — who?

YOUR SCORE

10

Make **Who** questions based on the answers provided.

1 Question : *Who is Joe's best friend?*
  Answer   : Andy is Joe's best friend.

2 Question : _____
  Answer   : Helen and Amy went to the library with Mike.

3 Question : _____
  Answer   : Mrs Kent is looking after the children.

4 Question : _____
  Answer   : Karen was on the phone just now.

5 Question : _____
  Answer   : Sue and Lynn go to school by bus.

6 Question : _____
  Answer   : Anne and I are in charge of the project.

YOUR SCORE

/10

PRACTICE $\boxed{D}$ Rewrite the questions and correct the mistakes.

1 Who fetching you from the office?

_____

2 Who like photography?

_____

3 Who was made this meat pie?

_____

4 Who have my postcards?

_____

5 Who be with your grandmother now?

YOUR SCORE

/10

_____

Underline the correct verbs in the questions.

1 Who (need / needs) a lift home?

2 Who (has / have) a spare pen?

3 Who (is / are) the newly elected prefects?

4 Who (give / gave) Liz that beautiful card?

5 Who (is / are) that man with your brother?

6 Who (expect / expects) to see Carol this afternoon?

7 Who (was / were) last year's Formula 1 champion?

8 Who is (go / going) to speak first?

9 Who (took / was took) my paintbox from the drawer?

10 Who was (hoped / hoping) to go on holiday this year?

YOUR SCORE

10

PRACTICE F Complete these questions using the words in the brackets and the correct words in the box.

is	was	attend	cook	play
are	were	attends	cooks	plays

1 Who _is your favourite singer?_ _____ (your favourite singer)

2 Who _____ (your favourite actors)

3 Who _____ in front of your house last night? (the men)

4 Who _____ in your family? (the meals)

5 Who _____ in your class? (the violin)

6 Who _____ in your neighbourhood? (tuition classes)

YOUR SCORE

10

UNIT 12.3 WH-QUESTIONS

what

Look at the **A** and **B** sentences below. Find out why **B** is correct and **A** is wrong in the **Grammar Points** section.

			GRAMMAR POINTS
1A	What did Anna **wanted**?	✗	
1B	What did Anna **want**?	✓	1
2A	What **you are doing** now?	✗	
2B	What **are you doing** now?	✓	2
3A	What **have** black spots and a growl?	✗	
3B	What **has** black spots and a growl?	✓	3
4A	What time **it is**?	✗	
4B	What time **is it**?	✓	4

GRAMMAR POINTS

1 In a **What** question, we use the verb 'to do' in this way:

What + the verb 'to do' + noun/pronoun + base form of main verb

Take note that the main verb must be in the base form and the verb 'to do' must have the right tense and must agree with the noun or pronoun in number.

EXAMPLES: What **does** Jane **like**? What **did** they **win** last week?
What **do** you **see**? What **did** he **say** just now?

2 We use the verb 'to be' with the 'ing' form of a main verb in this way:

What + the verb 'to be' + noun/pronoun + base form of main verb + 'ing'

Take note that, unlike statements, the verb 'to be' always comes before the noun or pronoun in questions.

EXAMPLES: What are they playing?

They are playing soccer.

What was Kim making just now?

Kim was making sushi just now.

3 We usually use the singular form of a main verb with a **What** question that is in the present tense. We often come across this type of question in the form of riddles and during quizzes.

EXAMPLES: What **has** a hump on its back?
What **eats** grass?

> **REMEMBER!**
> - **What** is used to ask questions about things and actions.
>   EXAMPLES: What is that?
>   What are you doing?
> - **What** can be used as the subject or object of the verb in a question.
>   EXAMPLES:
>   subject
>   What made you laugh?
>   **His silly jokes** made me laugh.
>   object
>   What did she make?
>   She made **a porcelain mug**.

106

4 We sometimes use **What** with a noun to ask for details about the noun. When the wh-word **What** is followed by a noun, the word after the noun has to be a finite verb.

EXAMPLES: What colour **is** your bicycle? ✓

What colour your bicycle **is**? ✗

What perfume **does** she **use**? ✓

What perfume she **uses**? ✗

What drinks **are** you **serving** at the party? ✓

What drinks you **are serving** at the party? ✗

PRACTICE *A* Complete the questions with **who** or **what**.

1 _____ machine is that? *A bulldozer.*

2 _____ did you break? *A teapot.*

3 _____ painted that picture? *Picasso.*

4 _____ day was it yesterday? *Monday.*

5 _____ writes well in your family? *Kathy.*

6 _____ is Ben's teacher? *Mr Collins.*

7 _____ are you buying? *Some lamps.*

8 _____ does that shop sell? *Office furniture.*

9 _____ stayed at your house last night? *Michelle.*

10 _____ is baking your birthday cake? *My Dad!*

YOUR SCORE
10

PRACTICE *B* Rearrange the words to form questions.

1 do — does — on — Saturdays — Sam — what?
What does Sam do on Saturdays?

2 are — eating — what — you?

_____

3 is — shirt — size — what — your?

_____

4 baby — holding — is — the — what?

_____

5 deliver — did — just — now — postman — the — what?

_____

6 do — in — keep — little — cupboard — that — they — what?

_____

YOUR SCORE
10

Circle the letters of the questions that are correct. There may be more than one correct question for each item.

1 A What colour is your new jacket?
   B What colour your new jacket is?
   C What is the colour of your new jacket?

2 A What gives you goosebumps?
   B What is give you goosebumps?
   C What giving you goosebumps?

3 A What do Marie usually have for lunch?
   B What does Marie usually have for lunch?
   C What does Marie usually has for lunch?

4 A What the athletes were doing just now?
   B What were the athletes did just now?
   C What were the athletes doing just now?

5 A What causing earthquakes?
   B What causes earthquakes?
   C What is cause earthquakes?

6 A What animal is that?
   B What that animal is?
   C What is that animal?

7 A What does the dolphins eating?
   B What are the dolphins eating?
   C What the dolphins eating?

8 A What do those customers wanting?
   B What do those customers wanted?
   C What do those customers want?

YOUR SCORE

10

PRACTICE *D* Complete the questions with the correct words in the boxes.

1 A: _____ John taking for the trip?
   B: _____ he plan to do there?

| What does |
| What is |

2 A: _____ the puppets?
   B: _____ she use to make them?

| What did |
| Who made |

3 A: _____ the manager of this shop?
   B: _____ you doing about our complaint?

| What are |
| Who is |

4 A: _____ Mary want from Taiwan?
   B: _____ Chinese silk too?

| What does |
| Who wants |

5 A: _____ his decision?
   B: _____ with him?

| What is |
| Who agrees |

YOUR SCORE

10

PRACTICE E Rewrite the questions and correct the mistakes.

1   What is the principal of your college?
Who is the principal of your college?

2   Who is the bestselling item in this shop?

3   What type of songs do Ken Rogers sing?

4   Who are you vote for as the chairman of our society?

5   What are exercises useful for strengthening the spine?

6   What paint you are using for the walls of your room?

PRACTICE F Write questions with the underlined words as the answers.

1   What *does Mr Lee own?*
(Mr Lee owns a restaurant.)

2   What _____
(The name of the restaurant is 'The Captain's Table'.)

3   What _____
(It serves seafood.)

4   What _____
(It opens at noon.)

5   What _____
(Its quick service and fine food make it popular with the office crowd.)

6   What _____
(Mr Lee is planning to introduce a buffet lunch at the restaurant next year.)

UNIT 12.4 WH-QUESTIONS

> answering **Who** and **What** questions – main verbs and the verb 'to be'

Look at the **A** and **B** sentences below. Find out why **B** is correct and **A** is wrong in the **Grammar Points** section.

CHECKPOINT

			GRAMMAR POINTS
1A	Who wants ice-cream? Tina and Susie **wants** ice-cream.	✗	
1B	Who wants ice-cream? Tina and Susie **want** ice-cream.	✓	1
2A	What are those things? **Those things** are shuttlecocks.	✗	
2B	What are those things? **They** are shuttlecocks.	✓	2a
3A	Who are you? **You are** Joseph.	✗	
3B	Who are you? **I am** Joseph.	✓	2b
4A	What are your hobbies? **Your** hobbies are reading and singing.	✗	
4B	What are your hobbies? **My** hobbies are reading and singing.	✓	2c

GRAMMAR POINTS

1 When we answer a question where **Who** or **What** is the subject of a verb, we replace **Who** or **What** with a suitable noun or pronoun and make sure the verb agrees with the subject.

EXAMPLES: Who **wants** sandwiches?

Rachel/She **wants** sandwiches.

What **broke** just now?

A crystal bowl **broke** just now.

Who **was singing** just now?

Sandy and Shane **were singing** just now.

What **is** in the oven?

Two chicken pies **are** in the oven?

2 When **Who** or **What** is **not** the subject of a verb, we usually do the following:
(a) change the noun in the question to a suitable pronoun and move it to the beginning of the sentence

EXAMPLES: **Who** is that woman ?

She is **Miss Hall**.
(complement)

> **REMEMBER!**
> ■ Normally, answers to wh-questions do not include **yes** or **no**.
> EXAMPLE:
> Q: Who has my book?
> A: Yes, Jane has your book. ✗
> A: Jane has your book. ✓

110

What are those flowers ?

They are **tulips**.
<u>complement</u>

What was Anita making just now?

She was making **jelly** just now.
<u>object</u>

(b) repeat the pronoun in the question

EXAMPLES: **Who** is she ?

She is **Miss Hall**.
<u>complement</u>

What are they ?

They are **tulips**.
<u>complement</u>

However, the pronoun **you** must be changed to **I** or **we** in the answer and the correct verb must go with it

EXAMPLES: **Who** are you ?

I am **Leela**. / We are **your neighbours**.
<u>complement</u>   <u>complement</u>

(c) change the possessive adjective **your** in the question to **my** or **our** in the answer

EXAMPLES: **Who** is your teacher?

My/Our teacher is **Mrs Lopez**.
<u>complement</u>

What is your occupation?

My occupation is **teaching**.
<u>complement</u>

PRACTICE A Rearrange the words to form questions or answers.

1 Question : drawing — he — was — what?

What was he drawing?

Answer : He was drawing a zebra.

2 Question : Who is your neighbour?

Answer : Graham — is — Mr — my — neighbour.

_____

3 Question : dogs — has — many — who?

_____

Answer : Diana has many dogs.

4 Question : her — is — staying — who — with?

_____

Answer : Her friend is staying with her.

5 Question : What fell on your car?

Answer : a — branch — car — fell — my — on.

_____

6 Question : carrying — just — now — they — were — what?

_____

Answer : They were carrying some sofas.

YOUR SCORE
/10

Look at the picture and answer the questions.

1 Who is playing with the cats?

_____

2 What is under the table?

_____

3 Who is at the door?

_____

4 What are Kim and Lynn holding?

_____

5 What is Faye's hobby?

_____

PRACTICE *C* Use the words in the boxes to help you answer the questions.

1 Who is that lady standing beside your car?   my mother's friend
She is my mother's friend.

2 What are those animals?   anteaters

_____

3 What is your favourite book?   'My Family and Other Animals'

_____

4 Who made that unusual box?   Maurice

_____

5 Who was with you just now?   my cousin

_____

6 What is in that basket?   some eggs

_____

1 Who organised the competition?
   A   The Speakers' Club who organised the competition.
   B   The Speakers' Club organised the competition.
   C   It was the Speaker's Club organised the competition.

2 What was the closing date of the competition?
   A   The closing date of the competition was 30th June.
   B   The date of closing the competition was 30th June.
   C   It was 30th June was the closing date of the competition.

3 What was the top prize?
   A   The top prize it was a box of leather-bound books and compact discs.
   B   Was a box of leather-bound books and compact discs.
   C   It was a box of leather-bound books and compact discs.

4 Who won the top prize?
   A   The top prize won by Colin Peters.
   B   Colin Peters won the top prize.
   C   Colin Peters was win the top prize.

5 What were the consolation prizes?
   A   What were compact discs and book vouchers.
   B   Compact disc and book vouchers were consolation.
   C   They were compact discs and book vouchers.

YOUR SCORE
10

PRACTICE $\boxed{E}$ Read the passage and answer the questions.

Beatrix Potter (1866 – 1943) was an English writer. She wrote books for children. Her books were mainly stories about animals. Her first book was 'The Tale of Peter Rabbit'. It was published in 1900. Her second book was 'The Tailor of Gloucester', published in 1902. Beatrix Potter was also an excellent illustrator and illustrated her own stories using watercolours.

1 Who was Beatrix Potter?
   She was an English writer.

2 Who read her books?

3 What were her stories mainly about?

4 Who wrote 'The Tale of Peter Rabbit'?

5 What was her second book?

6 Who illustrated Beatrix Potter's stories?

YOUR SCORE
10

UNIT 12.5 WH-QUESTIONS

> answering **Who** and **What** questions – main verbs and the verb 'to do'

Look at the **A** and **B** sentences below. Find out why **B** is correct and **A** is wrong in the **Grammar Points** section.

CHECKPOINT

			GRAMMAR POINTS
1A	Who does the ironing? Leah and May **does** the ironing.	✗	
1B	Who does the ironing? Leah and May **do** the ironing.	✓	1
2A	What does the clown have in his hand? He **have** 12 hoops in his hand.	✗	
2B	What does the clown have in his hand? He **has** 12 hoops in his hand.	✓	2

GRAMMAR POINTS

1 When we answer a question where **Who** is the subject of the verb 'to do', we replace **Who** with a suitable noun or pronoun and make sure the verb agrees with the subject.

EXAMPLES:

Who **does** the cooking? My grandmother/She **does** the cooking.

Who **does** the housework? Angie and Jason/They **do** the housework.

2 When **Who** or **What** is **not** the subject of the verb 'to do', we usually change the noun in the question to a suitable pronoun, leave out **do**, **does** or **did** in the answer and make sure the main verb agrees with the subject.

EXAMPLES:
Who **did** Tom **meet** at the library? He **met** James at the library. *object*

What **does** Karen **want** for her birthday present? She **wants** a racquet for her birthday present. *object*

Who **do** the children **like**? They **like** Mrs Gibson . *object*

What **did** the girls **buy**? They **bought** some books and stationery . *object*

Pronouns in the question are repeated, except for the pronoun **you** which must be changed to **I** or **we** in the answer.

EXAMPLES: What did **he** take?   Who did **you** see?
            He took my dictionary.   **I/We** saw the movie star Julia Robson.

114

PRACTICE $\boxed{A}$ Tick the correct answers to the questions.

1 Who does Janet study with?

☐ **A** She studied with Karen.

☐ **B** Janet does study with Karen.

☐ **C** She studies with Karen.

2 What did Richard keep in the tool box?

☐ **A** He keep the hammer in the tool box.

☐ **B** He keeps the hammer in the tool box.

☐ **C** He kept the hammer in the tool box.

3 Who does the grocery shopping in your family?

☐ **A** Dad and I do the grocery shopping in your family.

☐ **B** Dad and I do the grocery shopping in our family.

☐ **C** Dad and I does the grocery shopping in our family.

4 Who do the students want as their chairman?

☐ **A** They want Sally as their chairman.

☐ **B** The students want as their chairman is Sally.

☐ **C** They do want Sally as their chairman.

5 What do you take to the recycling centre?

☐ **A** I take old newspapers and magazines to the recycling centre.

☐ **B** I do take old newspapers and magazines to the recycling centre.

☐ **C** I took old newspapers and magazines to the recycling centre.

YOUR SCORE

10

PRACTICE $\boxed{B}$ Answer the questions by crossing out the wrong words.

1 What does Mr Lopez have?

He | ~~She~~ | ~~does have~~ | has | a motorcycle.

2 Who likes tea?

Mary | likes | liked | tea.

3 What does your rabbit eat?

It | Your rabbit | does eat | eats | carrots.

4 Who do James and John look like?

James and John | They | look | looks | like | his | their | mother.

5 What did Steve find?

He | Steve | did find | found | a camera.

6 Who does Gina visit on Sundays?

Gina | She | visits | visited | her grandfather on Sundays.

YOUR SCORE

10

PRACTICE $\boxed{C}$ Tick the correct words to complete the questions and answers.

1 What | do / does | your brother want for his birthday?

He | want / wants | a guitar.

2 Who | do / does | the gardening in your house?

My father | do / does | the gardening.

3 What did the children | has / have | for breakfast?

They | had / have | eggs and sausages.

4 | What / Who | do you need for your camping trip?

| I / You | need a compass.

5 Who | like / likes | Turkish food?

We | like / likes | Turkish food.

PRACTICE $\boxed{D}$ Answer the questions. Use the words in the boxes to help you.

1 Who do you wish to invite for our party? | Alice and her brother |

_____

2 What does Grandma want? | packet of tea |

_____

3 What does Ray plan to make this weekend? | wooden table |

_____

4 Who does Mr Weston hope to meet in Beijing? | old friend Mr Khoo |

_____

5 What do you and your brother usually give your mother on her birthday? | flowers |

_____

PRACTICE $\boxed{E}$ Read the passage and answer the questions.

Leslie Lopez went to Hong Kong in 1999 to study fashion design. While she was there she also modelled clothes for some agencies. During one of the fashion shows, she met a talent scout. His name was Richard Woods. He asked her if she was interested in becoming an actress. Leslie was thrilled when he asked her to go for a screen test. Leslie went for the screen test at a film studio and was immediately offered the role of the owner of a fashion house in a movie. The movie was a hit and Leslie received many offers to act. Leslie says she does not want to be an actress all her life. She gives herself another five years of acting and then she wants to try her hand at being a film director.

1 What did Leslie study in Hong Kong?

_____

2 Who did she meet during one of the fashion shows?

_____

3 What did he ask her to do?

_____

4 What did Leslie act as in her first movie?

_____

5 What does Leslie want to be five years from now?

_____

YOUR SCORE

10

PRACTICE $\boxed{F}$ Form questions about the words in the brackets based on the sentences. Use the verb 'to do'.

Larry wrote a postcard to David.

1 Who _did Larry write a postcard to?_ _____ (David)

2 What _did Larry write?_ _____ (a postcard)

Larry asked the hotel clerk for directions to the post office.

3 What _____ (directions to the post office)

4 Who _____ (the hotel clerk)

The hotel clerk gave a map to Larry.

5 Who _____ (Larry)

6 What _____ (a map)

Larry accidentally put the map into the letterbox.

7 What _____ (the map)

YOUR SCORE

10

117

UNIT 12.6 **WH-QUESTIONS**

where and when

Look at the **A** and **B** sentences below. Find out why **B** is correct and **A** is wrong in the **Grammar Points** section.

			GRAMMAR POINTS
1A	**Where your** mother?	✗	
1B	**Where is your** mother?	✓	1a
2A	**When he is** buying a car?	✗	
2B	**When is he** buying a car?	✓	1b
3A	**Where you will be** this afternoon?	✗	
3B	**Where will you be** this afternoon?	✓	2
4A	When did Tara **bought** the book?	✗	
4B	When did Tara **buy** the book?	✓	3

GRAMMAR POINTS ───────────────────────────────

1 We use the verb 'to be' with **Where** and **When** questions in these ways:

(a)   **Where/When** + the verb 'to be' + noun/pronoun

EXAMPLES:

Where **is** Madrid ?   When **is** your birthday ?
It **is** in Spain.   My birthday **is** on 19th October.

(b)   **Where/When** + the verb 'to be' + noun/pronoun + base form of main verb + 'ing'

EXAMPLES:

Where **are** you **going**?   When **is** Judy **leaving** for Japan?
I **am going** to the supermarket.   She **is leaving** for Japan in December.

REMEMBER!

- **Where** is used to ask questions about places, directions and locations.
  EXAMPLES:
  Where are Amy and Jane?   **Where** did I put my glasses?
  They are **in the music room**.   You put your glasses/them **on your head**.

- **When** is used to ask questions about dates and time.
  EXAMPLES:
  When was our last meeting?   **When** will we get our pay?
  It was **on 10th July**.   You will get your pay **on the first day of the month**.

---

2 We use **will** with **Where** and **When** questions in this way:

> **Where/When** + **will** + noun/pronoun + base form of main verb

EXAMPLES:

Where **will** ⟨Henry and Tina⟩ **go** tomorrow?   When **will** ⟨the professor⟩ **arrive** in Hong Kong?
⟨They⟩ **will go** to Venice.   ⟨He⟩ **will arrive** in Hong Kong on Monday.

3 We use the verb 'to do' with **Where** and **When** questions in this way:

> **Where/When** + the verb 'to do' + noun/pronoun + base form of main verb

EXAMPLES:

Where **does** ⟨Anita⟩ **work**?   When **does** ⟨the concert⟩ **start**?
⟨She⟩ **works** at a lawyer's firm.   ⟨It⟩ **starts** at 8 p.m.

PRACTICE ⟨A⟩ Fill in the blanks with **Where**, **When**, **Who** or **What**.

1 _____ is Dr Watson? *He is my uncle.*

2 _____ is Dr Watson's occupation? *He is a medical doctor.*

3 _____ does he work? *He works in his own clinic.*

4 _____ is the clinic? *It is on Holly Street.*

5 _____ did Dr Watson start his clinic? *He started it in 1995.*

6 _____ is the name of the clinic? *Watson and Lim is the name of the clinic.*

7 _____ is Dr Lim? *He is Dr Watson's partner.*

8 _____ did Dr Lim join the clinic? *He joined the clinic in 1997.*

9 _____ do the two doctors do after work? *They play tennis.*

10 _____ do they play tennis? *They play tennis at a club.*

YOUR SCORE 10

PRACTICE ⟨B⟩ Fill in the blanks with **Where** or **When**.

1 _____ are your parents? *They are in India.*

_____ will they be back? *They will be back next month.*

2 _____ are you flying off? *We are flying off tomorrow.*

_____ will you stay in Zurich? *We will stay at the Ritz Hotel.*

3 _____ are the essays? *I'm sorry. I haven't finished writing them.*

_____ will you give them to me? *I will give them to you tomorrow.*

4 _____ is my pet chinchilla? *I'm worried. I've been searching for her but I can't find her.*

_____ did you discover she was gone? *I discovered she was missing an hour ago.*

5 _____ did Jenny leave? *She left just a few minutes ago.*

_____ is the parcel she brought? *It is over there.*

YOUR SCORE 10

C Complete the following **Where** or **When** questions and their answers.

1 A: Where is your meeting?

   B: _____My meeting / It_____ is at the Orchid Hotel.

2 A: _____ you see Winnie?

   B: I saw her two weeks ago.

3 A: Where did Mr Thomas leave the keys just now?

   B: _____ them in that bowl over there.

4 A: _____ Patrick returning from Korea?

   B: He is returning from Korea on 30th May.

5 A: _____ Jessie and Ann meet us?

   B: They will meet us in the lobby of the hotel.

6 A: When do you want to visit Mrs Woods?

   B: _____ to visit her this evening.

YOUR SCORE
10

PRACTICE **D** Write **Where** or **When** questions for the underlined words.

1 Q: *Where do you live?*

   A: I live at 4, Ring Road.

2 Q: _____

   A: I will be at my aunt's place tomorrow.

3 Q: _____

   A: It (the train) will arrive at 1 p.m.

4 Q: _____

   A: I will telephone you at 6 p.m.

5 Q: _____

   A: They (the suitcases) are by the staircase.

6 Q: _____

   A: They (the guests) are coming at 7 p.m.

YOUR SCORE
10

Read the passage and answer the questions.

Jesse Owens was born in 1913. He was an exceptional American athlete. On 25th May, 1935, he broke six world records in 45 minutes at Ann Arbor, Michigan. In 1936, he won four gold medals — for the 100- and 200-metre races, the long jump and the 4 × 100 metres relay — at the Berlin Olympics. Hitler was so angry at the success of a black man that he left the stadium before Owens was presented with the medals. Owens' world record for the long jump remained unbroken for 25 years, from 1935 – 1960. He died in 1980.

1 When was Jesse Owens born?

   He was born in 1913.

2 Where did Owens break six world records in 45 minutes?

3 When was the Berlin Olympics?

4 Where did Owens win four gold medals?

5 Who was angry at Owens' success?

                                                                                          YOUR SCORE

6 When did another athlete break Owens' world record for the long jump?

                                                                                               10

PRACTICE F Form questions about the words in the brackets based on the sentences.

Janet is going to Paris on Wednesday.

1 Who *is going to Paris on Wednesday?*   (Janet)

2 Where *is Janet going to on Wednesday?*   (Paris)

3 When *is Janet going to Paris?*   (on Wednesday)

Kim studies French at the language centre every Friday.

4 What _____ (French)

5 Where _____ (at the language centre)

6 When _____ (every Friday)

He will meet Janet and Kim at the Louvre this afternoon.

7 Where _____ (at the Louvre)

8 When _____ (this afternoon)

                                                                                          YOUR SCORE

                                                                                               10

UNIT 12.7 **WH-QUESTIONS**

which and **whose**

Look at the **A** and **B** sentences below. Find out why **B** is correct and **A** is wrong in the **Grammar Points** section.

GRAMMAR POINTS

				GRAMMAR POINTS
1A	Whose these?		✗	
1B	Whose **are** these?		✓	1a
2A	Which painting yours?		✗	
2B	Which painting **is** yours?		✓	1b
3A	Which bus to your house?		✗	
3B	Which bus **goes** to your house?		✓	2
4A	Whose magazines you **borrowed**?		✗	
4B	Whose magazines **did** you **borrow**?		✓	3

GRAMMAR POINTS

1   We use the verb 'to be' with **Which** and **Whose** questions in these ways:

   (a)   **Which/Whose** + the verb 'to be'

      EXAMPLES: Which **is** Alan's house – the bungalow or the two-storey house?
                  The bungalow **is** Alan's house.

                    Whose **is** this?
                    It **is** mine/ours/his/hers/theirs.

   (b)   **Which/Whose** + noun + the verb 'to be'

      EXAMPLES: Which cat **is** Bob's?   Whose basket **is** this?
                  The grey cat **is** his.   It **is** my cat's basket.

REMEMBER!

- **Which** is used to ask the listener to identify or choose a specific item from a list that is known to both the listener and the speaker.

Take note of the differences between **which**, and **what** or **who**.

  EXAMPLES: **Who** is your favourite cartoon hero? (the possible answers are not known to the speaker)
                Which is your favourite cartoon hero – Superman or Batman?

                What school do you go to? (the possible answers are not known to the speaker)
                Which school do you go to – River View High or St. John's?

- **Whose** is used to identify the person who owns something or the animal that has something.

2   We use main verbs with **Which** and **Whose** questions in this way:

   Which/Whose + noun + main verb

   EXAMPLES:

Which student **won** the first prize – Ray or Kathy?   Whose house **has** arches?
Kathy **won** the first prize.   Mani's house **has** arches.

3 We use the verb 'to do' with **Which** and **Whose** questions in this way:

Which/Whose + noun + the verb 'to do' + noun/pronoun + base form of main verb

EXAMPLES:

Which movie **did** you **see**?　　　　　Whose umbrella **did** Kristy **use**?
I **saw** The Fellowship of the Ring.　　She **used** Annie's umbrella.

PRACTICE *A*　Fill in the blanks with the words in the box.

| What | When | Where | Which | Who | Whose |

1 _____ do you leave for Canada? *We leave for Canada on Friday.*

2 _____ birthday is it tomorrow? *It is Jack's birthday tomorrow.*

3 _____ camera did you use? *I used the old one.*

4 _____ has a new computer? *Susan has a new computer.*

5 _____ does Mr Cook own? *He owns a travel agency.*

6 _____ does your aunt live in Australia? *She lives in Sydney.*

7 _____ student wants to be the captain? *Robert wants to be the captain.*

8 _____ school has an environment club? *Ian's school has an environment club.*

9 _____ is your classroom? *The one next to the library is my classroom.*

10 _____ house did the thief break into? *The thief broke into Mrs Scott's house.*

YOUR SCORE

10

PRACTICE *B*　Underline the correct words to complete the questions.

1 Whose files (is / are) these?

2 Which person did you (vote / votes) for?

3 Whose dictionary is (this / these)?

4 Which teacher (do / does) Jan and Ian have to see?

5 Whose sisters (work / works) in Dubai?

6 Which is your (essay / essays)?

7 Which dog (bark / barks) all night long?

8 Whose song did the judges (like / liked) best?

9 Which (restaurant / restaurants) stay open till midnight?

10 Whose photograph (was / were) in the newspapers?

YOUR SCORE

10

Tick the questions that are correct.

1 Which bag yours is?

2 Which team lost to your team?

3 Whose secretary won the beauty contest?

4 Whose parents is on a world tour?

5 Which are your book?

6 Whose house did they buy?

7 Which channel do you want to watch?

8 Whose dog is Kathy's?

9 Which parcels are Tina's?

10 Whose are the furniture?

YOUR SCORE
10

PRACTICE D Write **Which** or **Whose** questions for the answers below.

1 Question : *Whose car had an accident?*

Answer : Kenny's car had an accident.

2 Question : _____

Answer : The singer from Spain won the competition.

3 Question : _____

Answer : Grandma's slippers are in the corner.

4 Question : _____

Answer : I borrowed Sue's raincoat.

5 Question : _____

Answer : That student hurt himself just now.

YOUR SCORE
10

6 Question : _____

Answer : I like the silver ones.

PRACTICE E Answer the questions. Use the words in the boxes to help you.

1 Whose son is an excellent artist? | Mr Norton's |

_____

2 Which art school did Allen attend? | Disney Art School |

_____

3 Which painting won the Grand Prize? | 'Miracle at Midnight' |

_____

4 Whose art gallery wants to buy 'Miracle at Midnight'? | Philip Dempster's |

_____

5 Which art competition did you enter?   ‘Artists of the World’

_____

PRACTICE F Study the diagram and answer the questions.

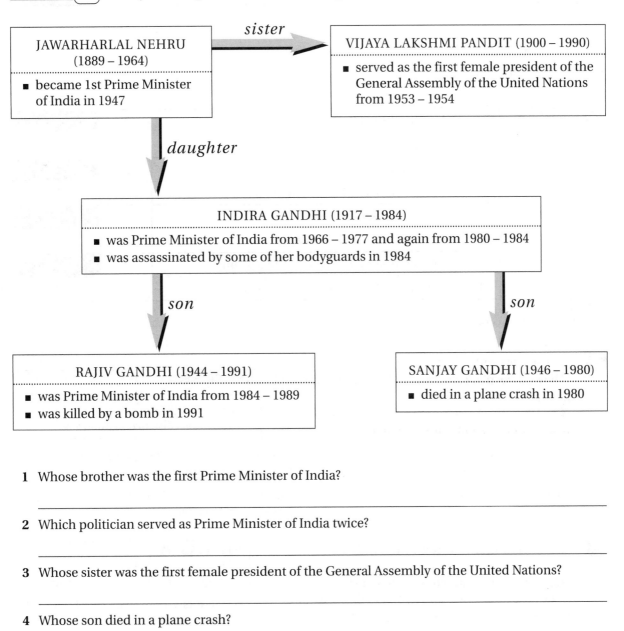

1 Whose brother was the first Prime Minister of India?

_____

2 Which politician served as Prime Minister of India twice?

_____

3 Whose sister was the first female president of the General Assembly of the United Nations?

_____

4 Whose son died in a plane crash?

_____

5 Which Indian politician was killed by a bomb in 1991?

_____

UNIT 12.8 WH-QUESTIONS

how, how many, how much

Look at the **A** and **B** sentences below. Find out why **B** is correct and **A** is wrong in the **Grammar Points** section.

GRAMMAR POINTS

1A	How old **these** trees?	✗	
1B	How old **are these** trees?	✓	1
2A	How much petrol **there is** in the tank?	✗	
2B	How much petrol **is there** in the tank?	✓	2
3A	How much salt **you need**?	✗	
3B	How much salt **do you need**?	✓	3
4A	How many **shop** here **has** alarm systems?	✗	
4B	How many **shops** here **have** alarm systems?	✓	4

GRAMMAR POINTS

---

1 We use **How** with adjectives in this way:

> **How** + adjective + the verb 'to be' + noun/pronoun

EXAMPLES:

How far is the bus station from here? (**distance**)
It is about two kilometres from here.

How old is your mother? (**age**)
My mother/She is 40 years old.

How big are the paintings? (**size**)
They are 60cm by 40cm.

REMEMBER!
- **How** is usually used with certain adjectives to ask for different types of information, for example, distance, age and size.

How long is the film? (**length of time**)
It is two hours long.

How tall is this tree? (**height**)
It is three metres tall.

2 We use **How many** or **How much** with the verb 'to do' in this way:

> **How many/How much** + noun + the verb 'to do' + noun/pronoun + base form of main verb

EXAMPLES: How many **magazines** did Gary buy?
He bought five magazines.

How much **sugar** do you take in your tea?
I take two teaspoons.

REMEMBER!
- **How many** and **How much** are used to ask questions about quantity or amount.
- **How many** is used with plural countable nouns, and **How much** with uncountable nouns.

3 We use **How many** or **How much** with the verb 'to be' in this way:

> **How many/How much** + noun + the verb 'to be' + **there**

EXAMPLES: How many **sticks are** there in the box?
There are 20 sticks in the box.

How much **paint is** there in the can?
There is one litre of paint in the can.

4 We use **How many** with main verbs in this way:

How many + plural noun + main verb

EXAMPLES: How many children **want** ice-cream?   (present tense)
Twenty children **want** ice-cream.

How many children **took** the test yesterday?   (past tense)
Twenty children **took** the test yesterday.

PRACTICE $\boxed{A}$ Tick the questions that are correct.

1 How old is this house?

2 How many children does they have?

3 How much salt did you use?

4 How much flowers did you buy?

5 How many flour do you need for this cake?

6 How tall the Eiffel Tower is?

7 How much work there is left?

8 How many people in your family like outdoor sports?

9 How much time do we have?

10 How far is our hotel from the airport?

YOUR SCORE
10

PRACTICE $\boxed{B}$ Rearrange the words to form questions and answers.

1 Q: grandmother — how — is — old — your?

_____

2 A: eighty — is — old — she — years.

_____

3 Q: does — grandchildren — have — how — many — she?

_____

4 A: five — grandchildren — has — she.

_____

5 Q: do — her — how — much — spend — they — time — with?

_____

A: They spend every weekend with her.

YOUR SCORE
10

Rewrite the questions and correct them.

1 How is your home far from your office?

_____

2 How many pairs of shoes you have?

_____

3 How many sugar there is in the container?

_____

4 How is expensive that antique urn?

_____

5 How many jars of jam you wanted?

_____

YOUR SCORE
10

PRACTICE D Use the words in capital letters to help you form questions.

1 Question : *How many postcards did Alina buy?*
  Answer : She (Alina) bought TWO postcards.

2 Question : _____
  Answer : He (Mr Gan) bought FIVE computers for his office.

3 Question : _____
  Answer : It (the museum) is ABOUT FIFTY YEARS old.

4 Question : _____
  Answer : We have A LOT OF money.

5 Question : _____
  Answer : FIVE students are absent today.

YOUR SCORE
10

6 Question : _____
  Answer : She (Sara) wants ONE KILO of flour.

PRACTICE E Read the passage and answer the questions.

Twenty men set out at about 4 p.m. that day to search for five-year-old Jamie who was missing. Mrs Kent, his mother, only realised he was not around the house when she gathered the children to have tea. The other three children were questioned but none knew where Jamie was. Cilla, the eldest, said she last saw Jamie in bed having his afternoon nap.

Everyone was in a state of panic. Mr Kent rounded up his workmen and explained what had happened. Then all the men went out to look for Jamie. Mr Kent took along their sheepdog Nikko.

It was Nikko that led the men to Jamie two hours later. He spotted the boy at the edge of the farm and barked excitedly. Jamie was standing in the stream. He had an empty milk bottle in his hand and he was trying to get some water into it. Nikko grabbed him by his shirt and dragged him out of the water. By the time Mr Kent got to Jamie, he was howling.

That night, Mr Kent made railings for the front door and back door so Jamie wouldn't run off and get hurt.

1 How many men searched for Jamie?

_____

2 How old was Jamie?

_____

3 How many children do Mr and Mrs Kent have?

_____

4 How much time did it take the men and Nikko to find Jamie?

_____

5 How many railings did Mr Kent make that night?

YOUR SCORE

10

_____

PRACTICE F Read the above passage again and complete the questions about the words in the brackets.

1 What time _did the men set out?_____ (at about 4 p.m.)

2 Who realised _____ (Mrs Kent)

3 When did Cilla _____ (having his afternoon nap)

4 Where _____ when Nikko spotted him? (in the stream)

5 How much milk _____ (none)

6 Which doors did _____ (the front and back doors)

YOUR SCORE

10

129

UNIT 12.9 WH-QUESTIONS

why

Look at the **A** and **B** sentences below. Find out why **B** is correct and **A** is wrong in the **Grammar Points** section.

GRAMMAR POINTS

1A	Why **you are** laughing?	✗	
1B	Why **are you** laughing?	✓	1
2A	Why **Macy ate** so little?	✗	
2B	Why **did Macy eat** so little?	✓	2

GRAMMAR POINTS

1 We use the verb 'to be' with **Why** questions in these ways:

(a) **Why** + the verb 'to be' + noun/pronoun + adjective

EXAMPLES: Why are the children tired?
They walked for an hour.

Why is he late?
He missed the bus.

(b) **Why** + the verb 'to be' + noun/pronoun + base form of main verb + 'ing'

EXAMPLES: Why is Kathy rushing upstairs?
She forgot to switch off the bedroom lights.

Why are they selling their house?
They prefer to live in an apartment.

2 We use the verb 'to do' with **Why** questions in this way:

Why + the verb 'to do' + noun/pronoun + base form of main verb

EXAMPLES: Why does Mrs Khan work so hard?
She needs the money.

Why did you miss the bus?
I woke up late.

REMEMBER!

- **Why** is used to ask questions about the cause, reason or purpose for something.

EXAMPLE:

A: My aunt is buying that old house on Sixth Avenue.
B: Why?

- **Why** questions can usually be answered by giving the reason straightaway. However, this is not acceptable in certain situations.

EXAMPLE:

Q: Why is she screaming?

(in a conversation)
A: She saw a mouse.

(in a written exercise)
A: **She is screaming because** she saw a mouse.

PRACTICE **A** Underline the mistakes in the questions. Write the correct words in the boxes.

1 Why <u>are</u> Charles on the roof?

is

2 Why do the students playing on the stairs?

3 Why does the boys always pull their cat's tail?

4 Why Jenny is crying?

5 When did Mr Avery goes to the club?

6 Why the students were cheering?

PRACTICE *B* Complete the questions with suitable words in the box. Each word may be used more than once.

What	When	Where	Who	Whose
Why	How tall	How many	How much	

1 _____ handwriting is this? *It is Mary's.*

2 _____ is Colin upset? *He can't find his keys.*

3 _____ soup is there in the bowl? *There is only a little soup in the bowl.*

4 _____ is Edinburgh? *It is in Scotland.*

5 _____ is your brother? *He is six feet two.*

6 _____ do you drink eight glasses of water a day? *Water is good for me.*

7 _____ do you leave for Thailand? *I leave for Thailand on 12th May.*

8 _____ bag is that? *It's mine.*

9 _____ did Dad get angry? *I forgot to feed the cat.*

10 _____ do the children like Mrs Johnson? *She is kind.*

PRACTICE *C* Complete the questions using the correct verbs in the box.

are	do ... eat	does	did ... call	is ... running
is	is ... climbing	did ... write	was ... staring	were ... shouting

1 Why _____ that woman _____ at you?

2 Why _____ you _____ the police?

3 Why _____ the boy _____ that tall tree?

4 Why _____ you _____ so much ice-cream?

5 Why _____ the men _____ ?

6 Why _____ Rosie visit the orphanage every month?

7 Why _____ the Environment Society _____ that report?

8 Why _____ the supermarket closed today?

9 Why _____ there so many cars parked along our road?

10 Why _____ the girl _____ away?

PRACTICE **D** Form **Why** questions with the verbs 'to be' or 'to do' using the given words.

1 Why / you / leave / the party / early / last night?
Why did you leave the party early last night?

2 Why / they / unhappy / now?

3 Why / you / banging / on the door?

4 Why / he / work with / Mary / this morning?

5 Why / Mr Ingram / take / bus to work / yesterday?

6 Why / you / limping / just now?

YOUR SCORE
10

PRACTICE **E** Rearrange the words to form questions or answers.

1 Q: he — shouting — was — why?

A: He was angry with his brother.

2 Q: Why did you chase the dog?
   cap — it — my — took.

A:

3 Q: are — sleepy — why — you?

A: I did not sleep well last night.

4 Q: Why is this chair wet?
   I — it — juice — on — orange — spilt.

A:

5 Q: does — evening — every — Ron — visit — you — why?

A: We play chess every evening.

YOUR SCORE
10

132

PRACTICE $\boxed{F}$ Read the conversation and answer the questions.

Mum : Sue, why have you been in your room the whole afternoon? Please come out.
Sue : I don't want to, Mum. I coloured my hair and I think I look awful.
Mum : Open the door and let me have a look.
Sue : Okay, promise you won't laugh.
Mum : Oh dear! Why did you choose orange for your hair?
Sue : I thought it would match my orange dress for the party. I'm not going to the party and I'm miserable.
Mum : Why won't you go to the party?
Sue : I'm afraid Rachel and the others will laugh at me.
Mum : Now, listen here. It's a costume party, right?
Sue : Yes.
Mum : Then your hair is perfect. Don't wear the orange dress. Wear something else.
Sue : Why?
Mum : It's not suitable if you're going to the party as a clown.
Sue : A clown?
Mum : Yes. Dress up as a clown. You will look wonderful. You can use Dad's overalls and we'll stick things on them.
Sue : What a superb idea!

1 Why does Sue want to stay in her room?

_____

_____

2 Why did Sue choose orange for her hair?

_____

_____

3 Why is Sue miserable?

_____

_____

4 Why won't Sue go to the party?

_____

_____

5 Why does Mum say that Sue should not wear the orange dress?

_____

_____

YOUR SCORE

10

UNIT 13 MODALS

can and may

Look at the **A** and **B** sentences below. Find out why **B** is correct and **A** is wrong in the **Grammar Points** section.

			GRAMMAR POINTS
1A	I can **jogging** for an hour.	✗	
1B	I can **jog** for an hour.	✓	1
2A	**I may** borrow your pen, please?	✗	
2B	**May I** borrow your pen, please?	✓	2

GRAMMAR POINTS

1   In a statement, we use **can** or **may** in this way:

> Subject + **can/may** + base form of main verb/the verb 'to be'

EXAMPLES: You **can/may** go out.   Susie **can/may** be successful.
            (subject)   (base form)   (subject)   (base form)

2   In a question, we use **can** or **may** at the **beginning** in this way:

> **Can/May** + subject + base form of main verb/the verb 'to be'

EXAMPLES: **Can** Joe stay?   **Can/May** I be your friend?
            (subject) (base form)   (subject) (base form)

REMEMBER!

■ Modals are a type of auxiliary verb. Examples of modals are **can**, **may**, **must**, **shall**, **will** and **ought**.

■ **Can** and **may** are used to ask for permission and give permission. **May** is usually considered more formal and polite than **can**.
  EXAMPLES: **Can/May** I use your calculator, please?
              You **can/may** watch TV after dinner.

■ **Can** and **may** are also used to express the possibility of an action or event. **May** is usually used to refer to a less likely possibility than **can**.
  EXAMPLES: We **can** have the meeting at 3 p.m.   (definite possibility)
              We **may** have the meeting at 3 p.m.   (slight possibility)

  May is also used to suggest that the speaker or writer is not very certain about something.
  EXAMPLE: Your answer **may** be right.

■ **Can** is used to refer to the ability to do something.
  EXAMPLES: She **can** swim well.
              Can you do cartwheels?

- Do not confuse **may be** with **maybe**. **May be** is a verb. **Maybe** is an adverb meaning 'perhaps'. It can also be the answer we give when we don't want to say either 'yes' or 'no'.

EXAMPLES: She **may be** late.   ✓   Will you be going to the prom?

   She **maybe** late.   ✗   **Maybe**. ✓

   Maybe she will be late. ✓

PRACTICE [*A*]   Circle the letters of the sentences which are correct for each situation.

1 Someone is interviewing you.
   A You can typing?
   B Can you type?
   C You can type?

2 You want to watch television.
   A Mum, may I watch TV now?
   B Mum, I watch TV now?
   C Mum, can I watching TV now?

3 You are worried about the weather.
   A It may rained on Saturday.
   B Maybe it rain on Saturday.
   C It may rain on Saturday.

4 You ask someone for help.
   A Can you help me carry this box, please?
   B Can help me carry this box, please?
   C You can help me carry this box, please?

5 Your games teacher wants you to try harder.
   A Can you be good at cricket?
   B You can be good at cricket.
   C You can good at cricket?

YOUR SCORE
10

PRACTICE [*B*]   Tick the sentences that are correct.

1 Mr Danker, may I introduce my brother to you?

2 I can have ice-cream after finishing my rice and vegetables?

3 This piece of news may be a shock.

4 Sometimes my little brother can be helpful.

5 We may completed our project by next Monday.

6 Can you stay underwater for a long time?

7 You may join any society in the school.

8 Can you repeated the question, please?

9 May be the motorist fell asleep while driving.

10 Can I speaking to the manager, please?

YOUR SCORE
10

Rearrange the words to form correct sentences and questions.

1 birds — can — far — fly — some — very.
Some birds can fly very far.

2 address — have — I — may — your?

_____

3 an — be — flower — may — orchid — that.

_____

4 can — I — leaflets — of — one — take — these?

_____

5 can — guitar — play — the — you?

_____

6 bicycle — borrow — may — my — you.

_____

YOUR SCORE

10

Fill in the blanks with the words in the box. Each word may be used more than once.

can	may	may be	I	you

Maria : Jackie, (1) _____*may I / can I*_____ borrow your calculator, please?

Jackie : (2) _____ return it to me as soon as possible?

Anna : Hello, Mrs Wong. (3) _____ speak to Helen, please?

Mrs Winter : I'm sorry. Helen is not in.

Anna : (4) _____ leave a message?

Paul : Good morning. I'm Paul Lim from City Bank. (5) _____ see the manager?

Secretary : He (6) _____ busy at the moment. Let me check.

It's alright. (7) _____ go in, Mr Lim.

Coach : David (8) _____ swim very well. He (9) _____ win the national swimming relay.

Meg : Steve, I (10) _____ help you with the school journal this

evening but I (11) _____ a little late.

YOUR SCORE

10

136

PRACTICE $\boxed{E}$ Fill in the blanks with **can** or **may**.

Visitors to Japan (1) _____*may*_____ be surprised to see how much the way of life there has changed. We (2) _____ see young people dressed in the latest American fashions. Soon fast food and 'pop' music (3) _____ replace traditional food and music.

The Japanese love for nature (4) _____ be seen everywhere. Japan (5) _____ be overcrowded but we (6) _____ still see small homes and flats surrounded by beautiful little gardens.

The Japanese have used their knowledge to show the world that they (7) _____ be leaders in trade and industry. They (8) _____ produce a variety of goods that are superior to those in many other countries. A survey (9) _____ show that almost every home in Asia uses some product made in Japan.

We (10) _____ learn a valuable lesson from Japan. In 50 years it has developed into a world power, a country we (11) _____ compare with any industralized nation.

YOUR SCORE
10

PRACTICE $\boxed{F}$ Underline the sentences that use the modals **can** and **may** incorrectly. Rewrite the sentences correctly.

Dear Len,

Thank you for the interesting letter and pictures you sent me. <u>I may see that you are a fine photographer.</u> You can write well too.

I can show your letter and pictures to a magazine editor here? She is looking for a talented travel writer and photographer. You maybe the person she is looking for.

May I ask you a question? I'm sure you'll say that I may asked you anything. Okay. I want to know if can I be a successful artist one day. If you don't think so, you can tell me the truth. I may trying another career.

Hope to hear from you soon.

Derek

1   *I can see that you are a fine photographer.*
2 _____
3 _____
4 _____
5 _____
6 _____

YOUR SCORE
10

UNIT 14.1 **PREPOSITIONS OF POSITION**

Look at the **A** and **B** sentences below. Find out why **B** is correct and **A** is wrong in the **Grammar Points** section.

			GRAMMAR POINTS
1A	The restaurant is **at** the basement of the mall.	✗	
1B	The restaurant is **in** the basement of the mall.	✓	1
2A	Dad isn't here. He's **in** the office.	✗	
2B	Dad isn't here. He's **at** the office.	✓	2
3A	The children are playing **in** the beach.	✗	
3B	The children are playing **on** the beach.	✓	3
4A	My house is **besides** a playground.	✗	
4B	My house is **beside** a playground.	✓	4

GRAMMAR POINTS

1   **at, in, on**

We can use the prepositions **at**, **in** or **on** to say where we live. We use **at** when we state the address. We use **in** when we state the town, city or country where we live. We use **on** when we state the floor or level of the apartment we live in.

EXAMPLES: I live **at** 4, Newton Road, New Delhi.
I live **in** New Delhi.
Pat lives **on** the second floor of Century Towers.

REMEMBER!

■ A preposition is a word that is placed before
   (a) a noun   EXAMPLE: The party is **at** Merlin Hotel .
   (b) a noun phrase   EXAMPLE: The cat is sleeping **on** the bonnet of the car .
   (c) a pronoun   EXAMPLE: I can't carry this box. There's something heavy **in** it .

■ Prepositions are used to express ideas such as **position** (above, under, in front of, behind), **time** (before, after, during), **direction** (across, along), etc.

■ The prepositions **in/on** can be used with the names of roads and streets.
   EXAMPLES: Mr Collins lives **in/on** Oak street.
             Matthew's office is **in/on** Darlington Road.

---

2   **at, in**

We use **at** when we want to show that a person or thing is at an exact location or a particular point. We use **in** when we want to show that a person or thing is inside something or in an enclosed area.

EXAMPLES: My mother is **at** the supermarket.   (not the post office)
My mother is **in** the supermarket.   (not outside it)

3 **in, on**

We also use **in** to show a person or thing below or partly below the surface of something. We use **on** when we want to show that a person or thing is just touching a line or the surface of something.

EXAMPLES: Jim's **in** the pool.
   There's a paper boat **on** the water.

4 **beside, besides**

We must not confuse **besides** with **beside**.

Beside means 'next to'.
EXAMPLE: The museum is **beside** an art gallery.

Besides means 'in addition to'.
EXAMPLE: She owns another boutique **besides** the one on Brooks Street.

PRACTICE **A**   Fill in the blanks with **at**, **beside**, **in** or **on**.

1 Mike lives _____ 25, Claxton Street and Sue lives _____ the house next to his.

2 He stood _____ a ladder to hang a picture _____ the clock.

3 Julie is _____ her grandmother's apartment. She and her grandmother often chat _____ the balcony in the evenings.

4 My brother likes to read _____ the garden. Sometimes, he sits _____ the branch of a tree and reads.

5 Richard and his family are _____ this photograph. Richard's father is standing _____ him.

YOUR SCORE

10

PRACTICE **B**   Complete the sentences with the correct words in the boxes.

1 The towels in _____*the bathroom*_____ are dirty.

| the bathroom |
| the floor |

2 Alice hung the wet clothes on _____ .

| the clothes line |
| the backyard |

3 The motorist parked his car beside _____ .

| the corner |
| the road |

4 Your scarf is on _____ .

| the drawer of that table |
| the top shelf of that cupboard |

5 Mr Davies left his briefcase at _____ .

| the bedroom |
| the restaurant |

6 The students are having a picnic beside _____ .

| the top of a hill |
| a lake |

YOUR SCORE

10

139

1 The umbrella stand is in a corner of the kitchen.

2 The fridge is beside the umbrella stand.

3 There is a kettle on the oven.

4 An ironing board is beside the oven.

5 There is a stack of ironed clothes on the ironing board.

6 A vase of flowers is on the table.

7 Mum is at the sink.

8 Sheila is beside Mum.

9 Bobby is in his pram.

10 Jim is at the window.

YOUR SCORE

10

PRACTICE $\boxed{D}$ Fill in the blanks with **at**, **beside**, **in** or **on**.

Martin, his mother and five other people were (1) _____*in*_____ a lift. The lift stopped

(2) _____ the fourth floor of the building but the door would not open. An old lady

(3) _____ Martin began to cry. A girl (4) _____ the back of the lift began to cry

too. One of the men banged (5) _____ the door of the lift to get attention. Another man

pressed the 'Help' button (6) _____ the switch panel of the lift. Martin stood quietly

(7) _____ his mother and waited.

Suddenly, the lift moved again. It stopped (8) _____ the fifth floor and this time the lift

door opened. Some security guards were (9) _____ the door to help everyone out. However,

the old lady refused to come out. She stood (10) _____ a corner of the lift and

faced the wall. Finally, two of the security guards brought a chair and persuaded her to sit

(11) _____ it. Then they carried the chair and the old lady out.

YOUR SCORE

10

My father bought a beautiful vase with paintings
of white storks (1) _____ it last month.
My favourite is the painting of a white stork
(2) _____ the air. It is such a graceful bird.
Did you know a stork can fly (3) _____ an
altitude of 4,000 metres?

The next painting shows a stork resting. When a stork
is (4) _____ the ground, it usually stands
on one leg.

Another part of the vase shows a female stork
(5) _____ a nest. There are two young
storks (6) _____ her. The mother stork has
a fish (7) _____ her beak. She is going to
feed her young ones.

This painting shows where storks build their nests.
Some nests are (8) _____ trees, some are
(9) _____ rooftops and others are even
(10) _____ telegraph wires.

YOUR SCORE

10

141

UNIT 14.2 PREPOSITIONS OF TIME

Look at the **A** and **B** sentences below. Find out why **B** is correct and **A** is wrong in the **Grammar Points** section.

			GRAMMAR POINTS
1A	I was born **on July**, 1988.	✗	
1B	I was born **on 21st July**, 1988. I was born **in July**, 1988.	✓	1
2A	I was at Tina's house **at Christmas Day**.	✗	
2B	I was at Tina's house **at Christmas**. I was at Tina's house **on Christmas Day**.	✓	2
3A	Our Sports Day **is on next Monday**.	✗	
3B	Our Sports Day **is next Monday**.	✓	3

GRAMMAR POINTS

1   **at, in, on**

We can use **at**, **in** or **on** when we give information about time. We use **at** to point to exact times. We use **in** to point to a period of time. We use **on** to point to a particular day or date.

EXAMPLES:

at 4 p.m.   (exact time)
at breakfast   (meal time)
at noon   (a point of time within a day)

in the morning   (a period of time within a day)
in July   (a month)
in 1999   (a year)

on Monday   (a particular day)
on Monday morning   (the morning of a particular day)
on 12th March   (a specific date)

REMEMBER!

■ The words **night** and **recess** refer to a period of time but they do not go with **in**. The word **night** goes with the preposition **at**. The word **recess** goes with the preposition **during**.

EXAMPLES:
Jean practises the piano **at night**.
I usually have a sandwich **during recess**.

---

2   **at, on**

We can also use **at** and **on** for specific events and occasions like public holidays. We usually use **on** when the event ends in the word 'day', and **at** when it does not.

EXAMPLES: Her sister got married **on New Year's Day**.
James threw a party **on his birthday**.

Jane visited her family **at Easter**.
He gave a speech **at the prize presentation ceremony**.

142

3 We do not use **at**, **in** or **on** before any of these words:
   each, every, next, one, last

   EXAMPLES: Fay and David play chess **on every evening**.   ☒

   Fay and David play chess **every evening**.   ☑

   My birthday was **on last Saturday**.   ☒

   My birthday was **last Saturday**.   ☑

PRACTICE A Fill in the blanks with **at**, **in** or **on**.

1 Labour Day is _____ 1st May.

2 The Art Society is meeting _____ 3 p.m.

3 I spent two months in California _____ 1999.

4 Many supermarkets are open _____ Sunday.

5 The train leaves for Paris _____ 1 o'clock.

6 My grandfather often has a nap _____ the afternoon.

7 My country celebrates its National Day _____ August.

8 Joe sent Mary 12 roses _____ Valentine's Day.

9 They usually meet at Donna's house _____ Saturday evening.

10 Our family always eats together _____ dinnertime.

YOUR SCORE 10

PRACTICE B Complete the sentences with the correct words in the boxes.

1 I had lunch with Jane _last week_____ .

| last week |
| Tuesday |

2 Winnie and Mike play tennis on _____ .

| every Sunday |
| Sunday morning |

3 I was in Spain _____ many years ago.

| one summer |
| on one summer |

4 Joseph has to finish the project in _____ .

| May |
| next May |

5 The hockey team left for Tokyo at _____ .

| last night |
| 9 p.m. |

6 Mrs Ford takes her dogs for a walk _____ .

| each evening |
| the evening |

YOUR SCORE 10

143

Tick the words in **B** that can go with those in **A**.

A	B
1 Kenny and his family go fishing on	✓ Saturday.
	✓ Saturday morning.
	☐ every Saturday.
2 Our annual concert is in	☐ July.
	☐ 29th July.
	☐ the afternoon.
3 The fireworks display began at	☐ midnight.
	☐ 11 p.m.
	☐ one night.
4 Sean always has a cup of tea	☐ at breakfast.
	☐ at 7 a.m.
	☐ in the morning.
5 We celebrated my sister's birthday	☐ last Sunday.
	☐ on Sunday.
	☐ in May.

YOUR SCORE

10

PRACTICE *D*   Rewrite the sentences and correct any mistakes in the use of prepositions.

1 I saw the mysterious figure in one evening.

_____

2 Our new house will be ready on April.

_____

3 Sean and his friends play basketball at every weekend.

_____

4 Mrs Stevens was in Colombo for a conference in last month.

_____

5 I have many clothes to iron on each day.

_____

YOUR SCORE

10

PRACTICE *E* Rewrite the sentences and change the time words to the ones in the boxes. Put **at**, **in** or **on** in the correct places.

1 We sold our house last year. | February |

We sold our house in February.

2 I woke up suddenly at 4 a.m. | midnight |

_____

3 The police arrested the kidnappers at 10 o'clock last night. | 21st May |

_____

4 Janet stays at home every Christmas. | Christmas Day |

_____

5 Richard intends to resign from the company in November. | next month |

_____

6 The ship sent out distress signals at about 5 p.m. | the evening |

_____

PRACTICE *F* Fill in the blanks with **at**, **in**, **on** or **–** (no preposition).

Sue Morgan woke up (1) _____ dawn (2) _____ 21st August. She was so excited she could no longer sleep. It was (3) _____ today that her first novel *Dark Moon* (4) _____ *June* would be launched at the Vista Hotel. Sue lay in bed until the phone rang (5) _____ 8 a.m. It was her absent-minded sister, Sally.

"Sue, is your book launch (6) _____ the morning or (7) _____ the afternoon?" she asked.

"It's (8) _____ 10 a.m., Sally," said Sue. "Please don't be late for it."

"I'll leave the house by 9.30 a.m.," suggested Sally.

"Please leave earlier. Remember the traffic jam (9) _____ last Friday? We were delayed for two hours," said Sue.

"Don't worry," said her sister. "I'll be there early…Sue, there's someone at the door. I'll have to hang up now. I'll see you tomorrow."

"Tomorrow?" asked Sue.

"Your book launch is (10) _____ 22nd August, isn't it? That's tomorrow," said Sally.

"No, it's today, Sally!" cried Sue. "Don't come for my book launch one day late!"

UNIT 15 PUNCTUATION

> apostrophe, capital letter, exclamation mark, full stop, question mark

Look at the **A** and **B** sentences below. Find out why **B** is correct and **A** is wrong in the **Grammar Points** section.

GRAMMAR POINTS

1A	I have two sisters. **their** names are Liz and Anne.	✗	
1B	I have two sisters. **Their** names are Liz and Anne.	✓	1
2A	What is on that wall**?.**	✗	
2B	What is on that wall**?**	✓	2a
3A	**Oh no.** The cinema is on fire.	✗	
3B	**Oh no!** The cinema is on fire.	✓	2b
4A	He **does'nt** want that book.	✗	
4B	He **doesn't** want that book.	✓	3

GRAMMAR POINTS

1   We begin a sentence with a capital letter.

EXAMPLES: **I**rene comes from Kenya. **H**er husband comes from India.
Where do you come from?

2   We use only **one** punctuation mark at the end of a sentence.

(a)   We usually use a full stop (.) for a sentence that gives information and a question mark (?) for a sentence that asks for information.

EXAMPLES: Henry wants to be an astronaut**.**
Where does Mr Johnson work**?**

(b)   We usually use an exclamation mark (!) after a word, phrase or sentence that expresses strong emotion such as surprise or anger.

EXAMPLES: Ouch**!** Watch out**!**
There is a spaceship in the sky**!**

> **REMEMBER!**
> - A sentence can take one of four forms:
>   (a) a statement
>   **EXAMPLE:**
>   I am in school.
>   (b) a question
>   **EXAMPLE:**
>   Are you in school?
>   (c) an instruction or command
>   **EXAMPLES:**
>   Draw a circle.
>   Don't touch the kettle.
>   (d) an exclamation
>   **EXAMPLE:**
>   Marie scored full marks in the exam!

3   Besides using an apostrophe to show ownership or relationship (see **Possessives**, page 18), we use it to shorten certain words. We do it in these ways:

(a)   verb + **not** = verb+n't (**'** takes the place of 'o' in **not**)

> such verbs include **is, are, was, were, do, does, did, has, have, had, must, could, would**

EXAMPLES: Fred **is not** joining us.   →   Fred **isn't** joining us.
I **do not** like coffee.   →   I **don't** like coffee.
You **must not** drive fast.   →   You **mustn't** drive fast.

(b) the verb **can/will** + **not** = **can't/won't**

    EXAMPLES: You **cannot** leave now.   →   You **can't** leave now.

                 Rina **will not** be here tomorrow. → Rina **won't** be here tomorrow.

(c) pronoun + **is/are/am** = pronoun + shortened verb

    EXAMPLES: **He is** Arthur.   →   **He's** Arthur.   (**is** becomes **'s**)

                 We are at the cinema. → **We're** at the cinema. (**are** becomes **'re**)

                 I am Susie.   →   **I'm** Susie.   (**am** becomes **'m**)

(d) noun + **is** = noun + shortened verb

    EXAMPLE: My **bicycle is** under the tree. →   My **bicycle's** under the tree.

PRACTICE | *A* | Tick the sentences that use punctuation marks correctly.

1 My parents aren't at home.

2 His coats on the chair.

3 ken borrowed our lawnmower yesterday.

4 You can't go near the cages.

5 I dont like impatient people.

6 Valerie's in the canteen.

7 Where are my hamsters?

8 Help. I'm in trouble.

9 That man's a thief!

10 Why didn't you telephone me yesterday.

YOUR SCORE

10

PRACTICE | *B* | Fill in the blanks with the correct words in the boxes.

1 _____ wants a _____

That boy	kite?
that boy	kite.

2 _____ That bus is going to hit _____

Look out.	you.
Look out!	you!

3 _____ my paint _____

Where's	box!
Where	box?

4 Carol and Anne _____ with me. _____ with Hannah.

aren't	They're
are'nt	Theyre

5 Your _____ a week away. You _____ forget to buy a suitcase.

holidays	must'nt
holiday's	mustn't

YOUR SCORE

10

147

PRACTICE **C** Rewrite the sentences using the correct punctuation marks.

1 Shes Janet Moor
She's Janet Moor.

2 Wheres the letter.

_____

3 he doesnt know how to boil an egg.

_____

4 Oh dear I cant find my bus ticket!

_____

5 Dont worry. I wont lose the money.

_____

6 The documents arent with me. Theyre with Christine.

_____

YOUR SCORE
10

PRACTICE **D** The mistakes in punctuation have been underlined. Circle the words with the correct punctuation marks in the boxes.

Martin :	Dad, look at the <u>dolphins</u>	**1**	dolphins?	(dolphins!)
	<u>Theyre</u> swimming around in the tank.	**2**	They're	Theyr'e
	They <u>dont</u> look wild at all.	**3**	do'nt	don't
Dad :	<u>we</u> call them bottle-nosed dolphins.	**4**	We	WE
Martin :	They seem to be smiling all the <u>time</u>	**5**	time.	time?
Dad :	<u>Thats</u> because of the way their mouths are curved.	**6**	That's	Thats'
Martin :	Dad, a tall <u>mans</u> on the plank over the tank.	**7**	man's	mans'
	Is he going to dive into the <u>tank?.</u>	**8**	tank?	tank.
Dad :	No, he <u>is'nt</u> going to do that.	**9**	isnt	isn't
	See, he's throwing a fish into the air.			
Martin :	Dad, a <u>dolphins</u> in the air!	**10**	dolphin's	dolphins'
	It's snatching the fish in its <u>snout</u>	**11**	snout?	snout!

YOUR SCORE
10

148

PRACTICE E Rewrite the sentences and shorten some words by using the apostrophe.

1 Kim is the best debater in our school.
   Kim's the best debater in our school.

2 Those boys are not interested in football.
   _____

3 James could not find his way to your house.
   _____

4 Mum, Aunt Mary is on the phone.
   _____

5 We are excited about the trip to Tasmania.
   _____

6 Mr Norton will not be attending the meeting.
   _____

PRACTICE F The mistakes in punctuation have been underlined. Rewrite the words using the correct punctuation marks.

1 the children haven't come down,

   John. Why is it so quiet upstairs.

   I wonder what they're doing?

   Im going to check on them…Oh

5 my goodness. Children, what are

   you doing? Youve got paint on your

   faces! No, you cant play Red Indians

   in the bedroom. please wash your faces

   right now, I want you downstairs in

10 five minutes. Dinners almost ready and

   Dad doesnt like to be kept waiting.

The

UNIT 16.1 SENTENCE STRUCTURE

joining two sentences with **and** and **but**

Look at the **A** and **B** sentences below. Find out why **B** is correct and **A** is wrong in the **Grammar Points** section.

CHECKPOINT

GRAMMAR POINTS

1A	My brother is a doctor **but** I am a lawyer.	✗	
1B	My brother is a doctor **and** I am a lawyer.	✓	1
2A	The sun was shining **and** the water was cold.	✗	
2B	The sun was shining **but** the water was cold.	✓	2

GRAMMAR POINTS

1 We use **and** to join sentences when their meanings go well together.

EXAMPLE: My father is an engineer. (occupation)
My mother is a librarian. (occupation)
My father is an engineer **and** my mother is a librarian.

2 We use **but** to join sentences when their meanings contrast with each other.

EXAMPLE: Mr Dass enjoys **fast** music.
Mrs Dass prefers **slow** tunes.
Mr Dass enjoys **fast** music **but** Mrs Dass prefers **slow** tunes.

REMEMBER!

- A sentence with only one finite verb is a simple sentence.
  EXAMPLE: I **like** music. (simple sentence)

- When two simple sentences are joined together using **and** or **but**, a compound sentence is formed.

  EXAMPLES: I **like** music. (simple sentence)
  She **likes** sports. (simple sentence)
  I **like** music and she **likes** sports. (compound sentence)

  I **like** music. (simple sentence)
  She **hates** it. (simple sentence)
  I **like** music but she **hates** it. (compound sentence)

PRACTICE $\boxed{A}$ Underline the correct words in the brackets to complete the sentences.

1 Nick is quiet (and / but) his twin is noisy.

2 Ashley did well (and / but) she received a prize.

3 I invited Ron but he (could come / could not come).

4 Russ tried to score a goal (and / but) he failed.

5 Lynn is a musician (and / but) her sister is an artist.

6 Mr Shane is reading and Mrs Shane is (drawing / friendly).

7 Jessie likes hockey and her sister (likes / does not like) it too.

8 The moon is full (and / but) it looks beautiful.

9 Tom is lazy but his sister is (hardworking / clever).

10 The house is large but the garden is (big / small).

PRACTICE $\boxed{B}$ Circle the letters of the best compound sentences.

1 Roses are beautiful. They smell sweet.
   A   Roses are beautiful and they smell sweet.
   B   Roses are beautiful but they smell sweet.
   C   Roses are beautiful, they smell sweet.

2 I have many neighbours. I like all of them.
   A   I have many neighbours but I like all of them.
   B   I have many neighbours and I like all of them.
   C   I have many neighbours, like all of them.

3 Sasha will clean the house. Enrico will wash the car.
   A   Sasha will clean the house but Enrico will wash the car.
   B   Sasha will clean the house and Enrico will wash the car.
   C   Sasha will clean the house, Enrico will wash the car.

4 Amin tried to repair the engine. He could not do it.
   A   Amin tried to repair the engine but he could not do it.
   B   Amin tried to repair the engine and he could not do it.
   C   Amin tried to repair the engine, he could not do it.

5 I looked for her in the staffroom. She was not there.
   A   I looked for her in the staffroom but was not there.
   B   I looked for her in the staffroom and was not there.
   C   I looked for her in the staffroom but she was not there.

PRACTICE $\boxed{C}$ Complete the dialogues using **and** or **but**.

1 Jeff : I've done what you wanted, Mum. I've swept the floor _____ I've washed the dishes.

Mum : Uh-oh! You swept the floor _____ you didn't sweep under the table.

2 Customer : That table is beautiful _____ it is too big.

Salesman : This table is beautiful _____ it is smaller than that.

3 Lester : I enjoy horseriding _____ my sister enjoys it too.

Thomas : I enjoy horseriding _____ I'm too busy to go riding.

4 Peter : I enjoy cooking _____ I hate cleaning up afterwards.

Adi : I enjoy cooking too _____ I don't mind cleaning up afterwards.

5 Jack : I'll go with you to the supermarket _____ I'll help you with the grocery bags.

Mum : Are you sure? You came with me last week _____ you refused to carry any bags.

YOUR SCORE

10

PRACTICE $\boxed{D}$ Join the sentences below by using **and** or **but**.

1 Cats are tame animals. Tigers are wild animals.

_____

_____

2 He cooked a new dish. Nobody ate it.

_____

_____

3 She shouted for help. A passerby stopped to help her.

_____

_____

4 The boys went to the movies. The girls went shopping.

_____

_____

5 Sally searched everywhere for her bracelet. She could not find it.

_____

_____

YOUR SCORE

10

PRACTICE E Tick the sentences that are correct.

1 Our players tried hard and the other team was stronger.

2 Beth was scared but she smiled at the dentist.

3 The picnic basket is ready and the sky is cloudy.

4 Grandma enjoys knitting but Katie likes it too.

5 The ground was rough and they had a bumpy ride.

6 It was their wedding anniversary and he sent her red roses.

7 He owns a restaurant but his son helps him run it.

8 Lapdogs are cute but they aren't very useful.

9 The sun is rising and we can still see the moon.

10 He longed to study music but he became a businessman.

YOUR SCORE 10

PRACTICE F Complete the letter by underlining the correct words in the brackets.

Dear Lucy,

I am writing this letter in a horse-drawn carriage **1** (<u>and</u> / but) I hope you can read my handwriting. Most of the time the ride is smooth **2** (and / but) once in a while the horses become skittish. Sometimes, too, the coachman takes corners too fast but I **3** (am / am not) afraid. I know he is very **4** (experienced / inexperienced) and he can control the horses.

I am trying new things and my days are **5** (empty / full). Life is **6** (boring / exciting) but it can also be dangerous. Last week I went boating with another tourist down a very fast river **7** (and / but) we nearly drowned.

Yesterday I learnt to cross-stitch and became quite **8** (bad / good) at it. The day before yesterday I tried to catch fish in a lake **9** (and / but) was unsuccessful.

I am enjoying myself but I **10** (don't miss / miss) you. Take care **11** (and / but) give my regards to your family.

Love,

Julia

YOUR SCORE 10

153

UNIT 16.2 SENTENCE STRUCTURE

joining three or more sentences with **and** and **but**

Look at the **A** and **B** sentences below. Find out why **B** is correct and **A** is wrong in the **Grammar Points** section.

			GRAMMAR POINTS
1A	This is an iris **and** that is a lily and those are roses.	✗	
1B	This is an iris**,** that is a lily and those are roses.	✓	1a
2A	I am Kit **and** he is Jim **and** she is Lyn and this is Jo.	✗	
2B	I am Kit**,** he is Jim**,** she is Lyn and this is Jo.	✓	1b
3A	The sky is blue**,** the sun is bright **and** the air is cool.	✗	
3B	The sky is blue **and** the sun is bright **but** the air is cool.	✓	2

GRAMMAR POINTS

1 (a) When the meanings of three simple sentences go well together, we can join them with a **comma** and then with **and**:

> sentence + comma + sentence + **and** + sentence

EXAMPLE: Dad jogs. Mum walks. Grandpa swims.
Dad jogs**,** Mum walks **and** Grandpa swims.

(b) When the meanings of four or more simple sentences go well together, we can join them with **commas** and then with **and**:

> sentence + comma + sentence + comma + ... + **and** + sentence

EXAMPLE: Dad jogs. Mum walks. Grandpa swims. Grandma plays badminton.
Dad jogs**,** Mum walks**,** Grandpa swims **and** Grandma plays badminton.

2 We can use **and** and **but** together to join three simple sentences.
We use **and** to join the sentences that go well together. We use **but** to join the sentences that contrast with each other.

EXAMPLE: sentence + **and** + sentence + **but** + sentence

She is shy. Her sister is quiet. Their brother is talkative.
She is shy **and** her sister is quiet **but** their brother is talkative.

Circle the letters of the best compound sentences.

1 I am in London. My brother is in Newcastle. My sister is in Exeter.
 A I am in London, my brother is in Newcastle but my sister is in Exeter.
 B I am in London and my brother is in Newcastle and my sister is in Exeter.
 C I am in London, my brother is in Newcastle and my sister is in Exeter.

2 I like spinach. She likes cabbage. He hates vegetables.
 A I like spinach and she likes cabbage but he hates vegetables.
 B I like spinach, she likes cabbage and he hates vegetables.
 C I like spinach, she likes cabbage, he hates vegetables.

3 Ducks quack. Geese honk. Goats bleat. Cows moo.
 A Ducks quack, geese honk, goats bleat, cows moo.
 B Ducks quack, geese honk, goats bleat and cows moo.
 C Ducks quack and geese honk and goats bleat and cows moo.

4 Zilla is a nurse. Julie is a clerk. Ursula is a teacher.
 A Zilla is a nurse and Julie is a clerk but Ursula is a teacher.
 B Zilla is a nurse, Julie is a clerk and Ursula is a teacher.
 C Zilla is a nurse, Julie is a clerk, Ursula is a teacher.

5 My mother is slim. My father is thin. I am fat.
 A My mother is slim, my father is thin and I am fat.
 B My mother is slim, my father is thin, I am fat.
 C My mother is slim and my father is thin but I am fat.

YOUR SCORE
10

PRACTICE B Fill in the blanks with **and**, **but** or a comma.

1 His hair was neat _____ his uniform looked smart _____ his shoes shone.

2 Jan cooks _____ Rose prefers to clean the house _____ she does it well.

3 Lightning flashed _____ thunder roared _____ a strong wind blew and trees crashed down.

4 I was tired _____ I wanted to rest _____ a visitor came.

5 He sang, she danced _____ I played the drum _____ we had fun.

YOUR SCORE
10

PRACTICE C Fill in the boxes with **A** where **and** should be, **B** where **but** should be, and **C** where a comma should be.

1 I shouted ☐ my mother screamed ☐ the fox ran away.

2 We dashed out of the house ☐ we rushed to the bus stop ☐ we waved at the bus ☐ it would not stop.

3 He'll have the mushroom soup ☐ she'll have the prawn cocktail ☐ my daughter will have the chicken soup ☐ I'll have the onion soup.

4 I have wonderful news ☐ my friends don't know ☐ I won't tell them yet.

YOUR SCORE
10

PRACTICE D Rewrite the sentences and form correct compound sentences.

1 Elaine cut the vegetables and I washed them but Elizabeth cooked them.

_____

_____

2 The bus crashed into a tree but the driver was injured and the passengers escaped unhurt.

_____

_____

3 I bought the cake and Amy chose the present, Sam made the birthday card for Mum.

_____

_____

4 This is Sue's sculpture but that is Larry's oil painting but those are my textile designs.

_____

_____

5 My dad is good at carpentry, my brother isn't good at it, I'm not good at it either.

_____

_____

_____

YOUR SCORE
10

156

E Underline the correct items in the brackets.

Mum loves shopping **1** (and / ,) I like it too **2** (and / but) Dad does not enjoy it at all. Dad walks into a shop **3** (and / ,) he sees something he needs **4** (but / ,) he points at it **5** (and / ,) he buys it. Mum and I go from shop to shop **6** (but / ,) we cannot find what we want **7** (and / but) often we do not even know what we are looking for. Dad laughs at us **8** (and / ,) shakes his head **9** (and / but) says we must be driving the shop assistants crazy **10** (and / but) Mum and I enjoy shopping too much to change our ways.

YOUR SCORE

10

PRACTICE F Rewrite the sentences, adding **and**, **but** or a comma where suitable.

1 I am quite good at squash he is more practised he is stronger.

_____

_____

2 The engine is coughing the doors are rattling the car is still running.

_____

_____

3 The story is exciting the stars are attractive their acting is good.

_____

_____

4 Cats and dogs usually fight your cat and my dog are good friends I love to watch them play together.

_____

_____

5 The curry was too hot the vegetables were too salty the rice was too soft.

_____

_____

YOUR SCORE

10

UNIT 16.3 **SENTENCE STRUCTURE**

relative clauses with **who**

Look at the **A** and **B** sentences below. Find out why **B** is correct and **A** is wrong in the **Grammar Points** section.

			GRAMMAR POINTS
1A	Priya is watching her niece who **swimming**.	✗	
1B	Priya is watching her niece who **is swimming**.	✓	1
2A	I know some girls they climb mountains.	✗	
2B	I know some girls **who** climb mountains.	✓	2
3A	He likes his classmates **who's** very helpful.	✗	
3B	He likes his classmates **who are** very helpful.	✓	3

GRAMMAR POINTS

1 When we join two sentences, we can turn one into a main clause and the other into a subordinate clause. Each clause has a subject and a finite verb.

EXAMPLE: We visited Mrs Tan. She was very friendly.

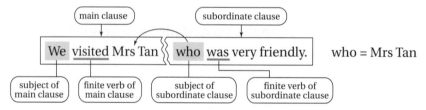

We visited Mrs Tan ⟩⟩ who was very friendly.   who = Mrs Tan

- subject of main clause
- finite verb of main clause
- subject of subordinate clause
- finite verb of subordinate clause

2 A relative clause is a type of subordinate clause. It describes a noun. We use a relative clause beginning with **who** to describe a person or people.

EXAMPLE:

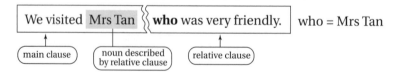

We visited Mrs Tan ⟩⟩ **who** was very friendly.   who = Mrs Tan

- main clause
- noun described by relative clause
- relative clause

REMEMBER!

- Simple and compound sentences do not contain subordinate clauses but complex sentences do.
  EXAMPLES: We visited Mrs Tan. She was very friendly.   (simple sentences)
  We visited Mrs Tan and she was very friendly.   (compound sentence)
  We visited Mrs Tan who was very friendly.   (complex sentence)

---

3 The finite verb of the relative clause must agree with its subject.

EXAMPLES:

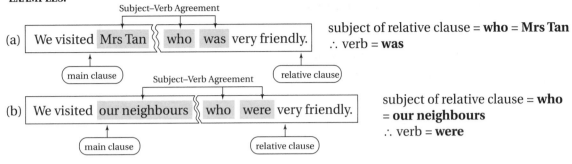

(a) We visited Mrs Tan | who was very friendly.

subject of relative clause = **who** = **Mrs Tan**
∴ verb = **was**

(b) We visited our neighbours | who were very friendly.

subject of relative clause = **who**
= **our neighbours**
∴ verb = **were**

PRACTICE | *A* | Underline the relative clauses.

1 I met some Japanese tourists who love spicy curries.

2 That is the officer who is on duty today.

3 Sally is a student who is very conscientious.

4 Janis and Joe have two children who are both very artistic.

5 This is the girl who won the oratorical contest.

6 The security guard caught hold of the man who was trying to break into the office.

7 I thanked the air stewardess who gave me some tablets for my headache.

8 Mrs Woods is the person who recommended you for the job.

9 I like our neighbour who always drops in for a chat.

10 He needs to talk to someone who can advise him about his studies.

PRACTICE | *B* | Underline the correct words in the brackets.

1 I met Miss Williams who (are / is) a lawyer.

2 Ming practises with Jon and Ravi (they / who) are fast runners.

3 We go to a doctor (he / who) has a clinic nearby.

4 Kit talked to the (worker / workers) who were resting.

5 I know a lady who (makes / making) the loveliest wedding cakes.

6 Linda is staying near a man who (has / have) 20 dogs.

7 We like (a dentist / dentists) who make our visits as painless as possible.

8 Ken is a man (he loves / who loves) old songs.

9 Lin has brothers who (are / is) very energetic.

10 That is the (boy / dog) who chased the thief.

YOUR SCORE

10

PRACTICE *C* Tick the correct sentences.

1 This is the chef who baked the cherry cake.

2 They know the man who live on the hill.

3 Asha visited her cousin he was not well.

4 We saw a lady was very beautiful.

5 We clapped for the athlete who won the race.

6 Ling and Ying are twins who like music.

7 I met some artists who is famous.

8 The bicycle belongs to Ian who is my friend.

9 We joined the women who is singing.

10 Miss Tanaka is the engineer who built that bridge.

YOUR SCORE

10

PRACTICE *D* Complete the sentences with relative clauses in the box.

who is a good listener.   who owns a boutique.

who taught us Chemistry.

who performed marvellously in yesterday's match.

who sold me the torn skirt.   who suspended two players.

who stopped the fight between two classmates.

1 She works for a friend _____

_____

2 They often consult Mary _____

_____

3 I complained to the salesman _____

_____

4 That is the goalkeeper _____

_____

5 Mervin was the student _____

_____

YOUR SCORE

10

Rearrange the words to form correct sentences.

1 one — campaign — she — started — the — the — was — who.

_____

2 cheering — fans — for — he — him — his — to — waved — were — who.

_____

3 book — everyone — for — is — succeed — this — to — wants — who.

_____

4 are — farmers — filming — harvesting — is — rice — she — who.

_____

5 at — barks — bicycles — dog — my — people — ride — who.

_____

YOUR SCORE
10

PRACTICE *F*   Rewrite the sentences to form correct complex sentences.

1 We spoke to a boatman he agreed to take us across the river.
   We spoke to a boatman who agreed to take us across the river.

2 Ted is one of the students who is organising the big walk.

_____

3 Sally comforted a little boy who crying for his mother.

_____

4 The factory had two supervisors were very strict.

_____

5 An astronaut is a person who travel in a spacecraft.

_____

6 It's Tim's idea so he is the one who have to explain.

_____

YOUR SCORE
10

UNIT 16.4 SENTENCE STRUCTURE

relative clauses with **which**

Look at the **A** and **B** sentences below. Find out why **B** is correct and **A** is wrong in the **Grammar Points** section.

CHECKPOINT

			GRAMMAR POINTS
1A	Len shouted at the dogs **who** were fighting.	✗	
1B	Len shouted at the dogs **which** were fighting.	✓	1
2A	A cat is chasing a squirrel which **running** up a tree.	✗	
2B	A cat is chasing a squirrel which **is running** up a tree.	✓	2
3A	David read the comics which **was** on the table.	✗	
3B	David read the comics which **were** on the table.	✓	3

GRAMMAR POINTS

1 We use a relative clause beginning with **which** to describe all nouns except people.

EXAMPLES:

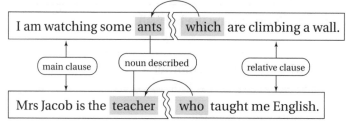

I am watching some **ants** || **which** are climbing a wall.

main clause — noun described — relative clause

Mrs Jacob is the **teacher** || **who** taught me English.

2 Like all clauses, a relative clause with **which** has a finite verb.

EXAMPLE: I am watching some ants which **are climbing** a wall. ✓

I am watching some ants which **climbing** a wall. ✗

3 The finite verb of a relative clause must agree with its subject.

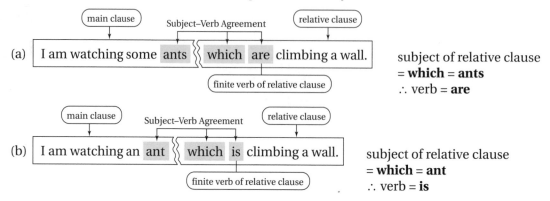

(a) main clause   Subject–Verb Agreement   relative clause

I am watching some **ants** || **which** **are** climbing a wall.

finite verb of relative clause

subject of relative clause
= **which** = **ants**
∴ verb = **are**

(b) main clause   Subject–Verb Agreement   relative clause

I am watching an **ant** || **which** **is** climbing a wall.

finite verb of relative clause

subject of relative clause
= **which** = **ant**
∴ verb = **is**

PRACTICE *A* Circle the letters of the sentences that are correct.

1 **A** Ben is driving a car belongs to Mr Raj.
   B Ben is driving a car which belongs to Mr Raj.
   C Ben is driving a car belong to Mr Raj.

2 **A** They play checkers which is an interesting game.
   B They play checkers which an interesting game.
   C They play checkers is an interesting game.

3 **A** We are listening to a bird which singing sweetly.
   B We are listening to a bird which are singing sweetly.
   C We are listening to a bird which is singing sweetly.

4 **A** Aida always wears dresses who suits her.
   B Aida always wears dresses which suits her.
   C Aida always wears dresses which suit her.

5 **A** I am arranging your roses which very lovely.
   B I am arranging your roses which are very lovely.
   C I am arranging your roses which is very lovely.

PRACTICE *B* Underline the correct words in the brackets.

Jo and Jeff are twins **1** (which / who) are very different. Jeff does not like the subjects **2** (which / who)
Jo likes. Jeff hates science which Jo **3** (love / loves). Jo is weak in English which **4** (are / is) his
brother's best subject. However, Jo is proud of Jeff **5** (which / who) speaks very well. Jeff is also proud
of Jo **6** (who / who is) a good sportsman. The boys quarrel about the pets **7** (which / who) they keep.
Jeff has rabbits which **8** (eat / eats) Jo's plants. Jo needs the plants for the experiments
which he **9** (do / does) at school. Jo has a puppy **10** (which / who) hides Jeff's slippers.

PRACTICE *C* Use the words in the boxes to complete the sentences.

1 Tim was made a director of the company_____

_____

father	his
owns	which

2 Help yourself to the apple pie_____

_____

bought	I	just
now	which	

3 They moved into the house_____

_____

beside	is	
park	the	which

4 I want a car_____

_____

expensive	is	
not	too	which

5 I do not like the remarks_____

_____

about	her	made
which	you	

163

PRACTICE *D* Complete the sentences with relative clauses. Use the words in the boxes and **which** or **who**.

1 The little boy watched the plane _____

| landing | was |

2 This is the man _____

| helped | us |

3 We admire the architect _____

| building | designed | this |

4 They caught the fox _____

| came into | house | our |

5 My pen pal lives in a village _____

| Bangkok | is | near |

YOUR SCORE

10

PRACTICE *E* Join the pairs of sentences. Use **which**.

1 We read about the stolen diamonds. They belonged to a rich banker.

_____

_____

2 My brother repaired our gate. It fell off its hinges two days ago.

_____

_____

3 I watched the deer. They were drinking at the pool.

_____

_____

4 James loves the carpentry set. It was a gift from his grandfather.

_____

_____

5 Sue leapt up and caught the balloon. The balloon was floating in the air.

_____

_____

YOUR SCORE

10

PRACTICE *F* Underline the mistakes in the sentences. Then write the correct words in the boxes.

1 Some countries have volcanoes which erupt from time to time. These eruptions kill hundreds of people which live nearby.

2 Last year Dora built a house which had a lovely view of the sea. Today Dora is staring at a condominium which blocking her view.

3 Our computer club is one of the school societies who have very keen members. Its president is a 13-year-old boy who is a computer expert.

4 We looked at the dark clouds that were gathering in the sky and welcomed the rain which they would bring. It would lessen the heat which making us feel tired all the time.

5 Ken joined some boys which were flying kites. They laughed at his kite which was crooked and comical but it turned out to be the kite which flew the highest of all.

PRACTICE *G* Rewrite the sentences correctly.

1 That team has players which is among the best in the world.

_____

_____

2 These are machines who will change our lives and this is the scientist which invented them.

_____

_____

3 I know a college which conducting very useful courses. They help students gain skills which makes them effective workers.

_____

_____

4 The mayor was staring at the fire which is destroying the city hall. His wife was thanking everybody who were helping to put out the fire.

_____

_____

5 Mum accidentally broke the bangle which to be my birthday present. She gave me another bangle which even more beautiful.

_____

_____

UNIT 16.5 SENTENCE STRUCTURE

adverbial clauses with **because**

Look at the **A** and **B** sentences below. Find out why **B** is correct and **A** is wrong in the **Grammar Points** section.

			GRAMMAR POINTS
1A	Nadya **works hard because** she does well.	✗	
1B	Nadya **does well because** she works hard.	✓	1
2A	I like elephants **it's because** they look gentle.	✗	
2B	I like elephants **because** they look gentle.	✓	2
3A	He was absent **because of** he was ill.	✗	
3B	He was absent **because** he was ill.	✓	3

GRAMMAR POINTS

1   We use an adverbial clause beginning with **because** when we want to give the reason for what is happening or what is stated in the main clause. An adverbial clause with **because** answers the question "Why?".

> **REMEMBER!**
> ■ The adverbial clause is also a kind of subordinate clause.

EXAMPLES:

main clause   adverbial clause

Dora is smiling ⟩⟩ because she has a new kitten.   ✓

verb in the main clause

Why is Dora smiling? Because she has a new kitten.   ✓

Dora has a new kitten ⟩⟩ because she is smiling.   ✗

Why does Dora have a new kitten? Because she is smiling.   ✗

2   We do not use **it's** before an adverbial clause beginning with **because**.

EXAMPLE: Flies are dangerous **it's** because they spread disease.   ✗

Flies are dangerous because they spread disease.   ✓

3   We do not use **of** after **because** at the beginning of an adverbial clause.

> **REMEMBER!**
> ■ Like all other clauses, the adverbial clause must carry a finite verb.

EXAMPLE: We stopped playing **because of** it rained.   ✗

We stopped playing **because** it <u>rained</u>.   ✓

finite verb

We stopped playing **because of** the <u>rain</u>.   ✓

noun

166

PRACTICE A Underline the correct words in the brackets.

1 She is successful (because / because of) she works hard.

2 He is wearing a cardigan (because / because of) he feels cold.

3 Everyone (dislikes / likes) Sheila because she is helpful.

4 They are (excited / jumping) because they are (excited / jumping).

5 We are sweating (because / because of) it is hot.

6 Mum is (pleased / sad) because we all feel well again.

7 We stayed at home (because / because of) the floods.

8 Mavin didn't buy the shirt because it was (new / torn).

9 I went to bed (early / late) because I was tired.

YOUR SCORE
10

PRACTICE B Rearrange the words to form correct sentences.

1 because — rested — tired — we — we — were.
We rested because we were tired.

2 because — played — they — they — well — won.

3 angry — Adam — because — he — shouted — was.

4 are — beautiful — because — flowers — I — like — they.

5 are — because — fat — love — sweets — we — we.

6 because — cat — hungry — it — mewed — the — was.

YOUR SCORE
10

PRACTICE C Rewrite the sentences that are not correct.

1 Mark did not have dinner because of he was full.

2 Our old car runs well it's because we look after it.

3 My grandmother is excited because of she is going on a holiday.

4 I like coconut trees because they are graceful.

5 She had a fever because she was absent.

YOUR SCORE
10

Tick the sentences that are correct.

1 ☐ **A** Dad's car broke down because he is walking to work.
  ☐ **B** Dad is walking to work because his car broke down.

2 ☐ **A** Tara lost her purse because she was careless.
  ☐ **B** Tara was careless because she lost her purse.

3 ☐ **A** Those towns are flooded because the dam broke.
  ☐ **B** The dam broke because those towns are flooded.

4 ☐ **A** Tina's employer was unfair because Tina quit her job.
  ☐ **B** Tina quit her job because her employer was unfair.

5 ☐ **A** That supermarket is popular because it offers a variety of goods.
  ☐ **B** That supermarket offers a variety of goods because it is popular.

YOUR SCORE
10

PRACTICE **E** Rearrange the words in the boxes to form adverbial clauses.

1 Many golfers like King's Beach and Golf Resort
_____

_____

| beautiful | | are |
| because | surroundings | its |

2 They also like the place
_____

_____

| accommodation | because |
| is | reasonable | the |

3 Golfers find the first nine holes of the course easy
_____

_____

| because | flat | is | land | the |

4 Many golfers practise their strokes daily
_____

_____

| because | improve | their game |
| they | to | want |

5 Some golfers can even practise at night
_____

_____

| because | course |
| is | the | well-lit |

YOUR SCORE
10

PRACTICE F Circle the letters of the sentences that are correct. There may be more than one answer for each question.

1 A My stomach is flat because I exercise regularly.
   B Your stomach bulges because you don't exercise.
   C I exercise regularly because my stomach is flat.

2 A The boat capsized it's because the sea was rough.
   B The boat capsized because of the sea was rough.
   C The boat capsized because the sea was rough.

3 A We can't sleep because we are too excited.
   B We can't sleep because of too much excitement.
   C We can't sleep because it's all too exciting.

4 A He fell sick because he did not have sufficient rest.
   B He fell sick because he did not have enough rest.
   C He fell sick because of insufficient rest.

5 A She is trusted because she often tells lies.
   B She is distrusted because she often tells lies.
   C She often tells lies because she is distrusted.

YOUR SCORE
10

PRACTICE G Fill in the blanks with the words in the box.

air	because	dirty	don't	is
it's	of	passes	silly	smart

Child : Dad, why can't we play outside now?

Dad : We can't do that (1) _____ (2) _____ raining.

Child : Why can't we play in the rain?

Dad : Most people don't do that because they (3) _____ want to fall sick.

Child : Why does playing in the rain make us fall sick?

Dad : It does that because rain water (4) _____ (5) _____ nowadays.

Child : Why is rain water dirty?

Dad : It's dirty because it (6) _____ through dirty (7) _____ .

Child : Why is the air dirty?

Dad : The air is dirty because (8) _____ the smoke from factories, cars and cigarettes. That's why I stopped smoking.

Child : But Dad, why did you start smoking?

Dad : I did that because I was young and (9) _____ .

Child : I'm young. Why aren't I silly?

Dad : You aren't silly because you have a (10) _____ Dad who won't let you play in the rain!

YOUR SCORE
10

TEST 1

A   Fill in the blanks with **a, an** or **the**.

Something unusual happened while I was at (1) _____ Royal Sports Club this evening. I was drinking (2) _____ cup of tea at the cafe when (3) _____ well-dressed couple walked in. (4) _____ man wore (5) _____ suit and (6) _____ woman had on (7) _____ satin dress. She carried (8) _____ umbrella in one hand. They sat nearby and began talking to each other. The woman stood up suddenly and shouted at her friend. He yelled back and soon (9) _____ argument broke out. Everyone in (10) _____ room looked at them.

YOUR SCORE

10

B   Rewrite these sentences using **'s** or **'** in the correct places.

1   The ladies committee decided to hold their food fair next week.

_____

_____

2   Mrs Tans youngest grandchild is a chubby four-month-old boy.

_____

_____

3   The cheetahs long slender legs enable the animal to run at great speed.

_____

_____

4   My best friend aunt is a well-known criminal lawyer.

_____

_____

5   The two lost sheeps bleats were heard by the shepherd.

_____

_____

YOUR SCORE

5

C Underline the correct words.

Patrick is a young seaman in the navy. **1** (He / She) is a gunnery officer on a submarine.
2 (His / Her) work is difficult and dangerous. **3** (He / It) keeps him away from his **4** (husband / wife)
and two children for about six months of the year. Carl and Kris miss their **5** (father / mother) very
much and wait for him to come home on leave.

YOUR SCORE
5

D Fill in the blanks by circling the correct words.

1 My grandparents are over 80 years old. _____ are still active and keep busy all the time.
   A He   **B** She   **C** They   **D** We

2 Betty and _____ are playing tennis at the club today. I booked the court yesterday.
   A I   **B** him   **C** her   **D** me

3 Our form teacher is annoyed with _____ for not passing up our homework.
   A her   **B** him   **C** us   **D** you

4 Vicki sat down beside me and placed her bag next to _____ .
   A hers   **B** his   **C** ours   **D** mine

5 The eagle swoops suddenly from high up in the sky to snatch _____ prey.
   A her   **B** his   **C** their   **D** its

6 These files are not mine. _____ over there belong to me.
   A These   **B** Those   **C** This   **D** That

7 The boys spent all _____ pocket money at the fun fair.
   A his   **B** her   **C** my   **D** their

8 I asked _____ to take the cake out of the oven but you forgot. Now the cake is burnt.
   A him   **B** you   **C** her   **D** them

9 Come over here and look at _____ furniture. I bought it recently.
   A this   **B** that   **C** these   **D** those

10 Paris is a beautiful city. _____ has several museums which contain some of the world's best
paintings.
   A It   **B** He   **C** She   **D** They

YOUR SCORE
10

Cross out the incorrect words.

The little ones watched **1** (intent / intently) as the magician began his show. He pulled out a **2** (red white large / large red and white) handkerchief from his trouser pocket. He folded it into a small square and put it **3** (deep / deeply) into his coat pocket. Then he took off his **4** (black, big / big black) hat and showed them two white doves inside it. The children were surprised.

They looked even **5** (more surprised / most surprised) when the magician began to pull the red and white handkerchief out of his mouth. The **6** (better / best) part of the performance was when the magician put a burning torch into his mouth. He moaned **7** (loud / loudly) to make it seem as if he was suffering. Then he smiled **8** (triumphant / triumphantly) and removed the torch to show that it was still burning **9** (bright / brightly). The audience clapped **10** (joyful / joyfully) as the performance ended.

YOUR SCORE
10

F Underline the correct words.

1 The girls (work / works) in shifts at the canning factory.

2 My father and his workmen (is renovating / are renovating) the house this week.

3 The accounts clerk (aren't / isn't) in his office so we have to wait for our receipts.

4 My friend (don't / doesn't) need my help this week.

5 Aunt Penny (don't / doesn't) want us to disturb her when she is cooking.

6 You (don't / doesn't) understand her problem so you can't advise her.

7 (Are / Is) the apple pie in the fridge?

8 (Do / Does) your sister have a microwave oven?

9 (Do / Does) your parents know about the accident?

10 (Are / Is) there enough detergent to wash all the clothes?

YOUR SCORE
10

TEST 2

Units 8 – 12

A In each sentence, the symbol ⋏ shows where a word or a group of words is missing. Rewrite the sentence and replace ⋏ with the correct word or words in the box.

1 Rabbits are very cute ⋏. | animals | in the home |

_____

2 They ⋏ the stolen goods here. | are | hid |

_____

3 You ⋏ write a letter of thanks to your host. | have to | to |

_____

4 Dad and I play ⋏ every Sunday. | on | volleyball |

_____

5 I found a silver bracelet ⋏. | ring | under the sofa |

_____

6 The dogs ⋏ furiously at a stranger. | are barking | barking |

_____

7 Jonathan is a very active ⋏. | child | nowadays |

_____

8 Everyone is ⋏ here on time. | be | to be |

_____

9 Janet and I ⋏ learning Spanish. | are | want |

_____

10 Brian's latest painting is ⋏. | boats | excellent |

_____

YOUR SCORE

10

B Underline the correct words in the brackets.

I **1** (am sitting / sitting) beside a Dutch lady on a plane to Amsterdam, Holland. She **2** (has / have) friends there. They **3** (know / knowing) she **4** (coming / is coming) and some of them **5** (will be / to be) at the airport to meet her. I **6** (feel / feeling) happy for her but sorry for myself. My friend Tony **7** (will meet / was to meet) me but he **8** (had to flew / had to fly) to London with his boss. Never mind, I **9** (am / will be) going to have fun and make new friends. The lady beside me **10** (is / was) already my friend.

YOUR SCORE
/10

C Fill in the blanks with the correct forms of the verbs in the brackets.

(a) Every Saturday night my mother (1) _____ (knead) dough to make fresh bread for the family on Sunday morning. Her bread (2) _____ (be) always good.

(b) At 9 o'clock last night, Jean (3) _____ (take) a shower. Suddenly the lights (4) _____ (go) out. She (5) _____ (shriek) and (6) _____ (drop) the bar of soap she was holding. Jean (7) _____ (kneel) on the bathroom floor and searched in the dark for about 10 minutes till she found her soap.

(c) Now we (8) _____ (pack) our clothes. At this time tomorrow we (9) _____ (board) the plane for New York. I know we (10) _____ (going to) have a wonderful time there.

YOUR SCORE
/10

D Fill in the blanks with question tags. Use the words in Box One and Box Two to form the question tags. Each word may be used more than once.

Box One	**Box Two**
aren't isn't	he I it she they we you

1 You and I are eating too much junk food, _____ ?
2 Her guardian's name is James Lee, _____ ?
3 You and your friends are enjoying the party, _____ ?
4 I am quite good at organising parties, _____ ?
5 One of the speakers is our teacher's daughter, _____ ?

YOUR SCORE
/5

Complete the wh-questions to match the answers.

1 A : _____ did Val come home?
   B : She came home this evening.

2 A : What _____ Keith do in his spare time?
   B : He makes his own greeting cards.

3 A : _____ pearl necklace is that?
   B : It is mine.

4 A : Where _____ you _____ my wallet?
   B : I left it in my briefcase.

YOUR SCORE
5

F Read the passage and answer the questions on it.

In prehistoric times, men hunted wild horses solely for food. Later, they hunted these animals to tame or domesticate them so that they would be useful. These domestic horses ploughed fields, carried goods, rounded up cattle and transported people from place to place. Horses were used in wartime too to carry soldiers into battle.

Horses are wonderful animals. They serve their masters well. There are some interesting horses in history that were well-loved and honoured by their owners. Alexander the Great's favourite horse was named Bucephalus. He had tamed the horse himself when he was a boy. The horse went everywhere with him on his campaigns until it died after a battle in 326 BC. Another horse, Copenhagen, was owned by the Duke of Wellington. When it died, he had it buried with military honours. Sometimes, however, horse owners can overdo their fondness for their horses. The Roman Emperor Caligula, for instance, made his horse Incitatus a senator!

1 When did men hunt wild horses solely for food?

   _____

2 What did domestic horses do?

   _____

   _____

3 Who used horses in wartime?

   _____

4 Which horse died after a battle in 326 BC?

   _____

5 Whose horse held a position in the Roman Senate?

YOUR SCORE
10

   _____

175

TEST 3

A   Fill in the blanks with the correct items in the box.

> at   beside   in   on   –

One morning (1) _____ last month, I sat (2) _____ a hilltop waiting for sunrise. (3) _____ about 6.30 a.m., my friend Paul came up the hill to meet me. He carried a rucksack (4) _____ one hand. Paul sat down (5) _____ me and together we saw the sun come up. Everything was peaceful and quiet. There was dew (6) _____ the blades of grass. Birds were beginning to chirp. Down below, some people were waiting (7) _____ the side of the road for a bus to come along.

Then we saw some birds (8) _____ the air, circling round and round. A squirrel stopped (9) _____ Paul and made funny noises. We made the same noises and it ran away. We had such a wonderful time that morning that we agreed to meet there again (10) _____ next week.

YOUR SCORE

10

B   Rewrite the sentences with the correct punctuation marks.

1 my uncle and aunt are interior decorators.

_____

2 Why didn't you return my phone call.

_____

3 Johns sketch of the river is excellent.

_____

4 Those are'nt the chairs I ordered from your store.

_____

5 My mothers not free to come to the phone right now.

_____

YOUR SCORE

5

Underline the correct words in the brackets.

Customer : **1** (Can / May) you bring me a glass of goat's milk, please?

Waiter : I'm sorry, Sir. We don't have it. I **2** (can / may) give you fresh cow's milk if you like.

Customer : No, thanks. **3** (Anyone here can / Can anyone here) find me a goat?

Waiter : The farmer over there **4** (can / may) be able to help you. He rears goats.

Customer : Thanks. I'll ask him if I may **5** (rent / renting) one of his goats.

YOUR SCORE
5

D Tick the sentences that are correct.

1 I spoke to her but she said nothing.

2 The bomb fell on the building but nobody was hurt.

3 Dad yelled at the cat, the cat just looked at him.

4 His hearing is good, his eyesight is excellent and his teeth are rotten.

5 You are a steady worker and you will succeed.

6 We fired, they ran and we chased them but they got away.

7 It is midnight but I am sleepy.

8 News of the incident spreading fast and everyone was interested.

9 She walked up to the house and knocked on the door but someone opened it.

10 He was seriously ill but now he is fine.

YOUR SCORE
10

E Rewrite the sentences and put in **because**, **which** or **who**.

1 The village had a rowing team won several races.

_____

_____

2 We remember her her drama classes were delightful.

_____

_____

3 Jane is a circus trainer teaches elephants to dance.

_____

_____

4 My neighbour says his plants grow well he talks to them.

_____

_____

5 He is the captain of the ship will sail to India tonight.

_____

_____

6 Mr Hall is the architect designed my neighbour's bungalow.

_____

_____

7 She didn't get the job she didn't have the necessary qualifications.

_____

_____

8 This is the vacuum cleaner is the lightest and most efficient in the market.

_____

_____

9 Please point out the sales assistant was discourteous to you.

_____

_____

10 All of us love the song made Rick Jones a singing sensation overnight.

_____

_____

| _F_ | Underline the sentences that are incorrect and rewrite them correctly.

Choosing the right home is something which is difficult to do. It is especially hard for my family because of we all like different things. My father is a person he needs a lot of space. He goes for houses which my mother calls palaces. My mother prefers small houses. It is easy to keep clean because she wants one. My brother is an art student who admires buildings with interesting designs. He would like a house like his friend's who looks really striking. My sister wants a flat that is ordinary and cheap. My dream house is one of those cottages which is found in the countryside.

1 _____

2 _____

3 _____

4 _____

5 _____

TEST 4

A Fill each blank with the most suitable word.

The kingfisher is a brightly-coloured bird with a large head and a long beak. (1) _____ tail, wings and legs are usually short. It (2) _____ near streams, ponds and in coastal areas. It (3) _____ fish and small aquatic creatures. You can often (4) _____ it on a branch above water waiting for (5) _____ prey. When it spots a fish, for instance, (6) _____ plunges into the water and grabs it in (7) _____ beak.

There are about 90 species of (8) _____ . The largest of them is the kookaburra. It (9) _____ native to Australia and lives in the bush. (10) _____ kookaburra is noted for its loud, laughing cry. It is known as the 'bushman's clock' because its call can be heard early in the morning and just after the sun has set.

YOUR SCORE

10

B Read the passage below and answer the questions.

My ambition is to sail solo around the world before I reach the age of 40. I'm only 15 now but I have lots of experience being at sea. My father owns a boat and he taught me a lot of things about boating. I know how to steer a boat, how to read the compass as well as what to do in emergencies.

Dad says if I want to go round the world, I must buy my own boat. I have accepted his challenge. In December last year, I started my 'Buy a Boat' fund. I save half my pocket money each month and I go around the neighbourhood to get odd jobs such as mowing the lawn, painting walls and running errands.

1 What is the writer's ambition?

_____

_____

2 How old is he now?

_____

3 Who taught the writer about boating?

_____

4 When did he start a fund?

_____

5 Where does he go to get odd jobs?

YOUR SCORE

10

_____

C Circle the letters of the correct answers to complete the passage below.

In many countries long ago, if you were born a girl, you (1) _____ to school. You stayed at home and (2) _____ to cook, sew and look after babies. While your brother was studying for (3) _____ occupation, you (4) _____ to become (5) _____ housewife and mother. If you were lucky, you (6) _____ a tutor to give you (7) _____ education at home. But even if you were much (8) _____ than your brother, (9) _____ was the one who had a chance to go to the university. For you, the road to the university had a 'No Entry' sign in (10) _____ letters.

Nowadays, girls and boys (11) _____ equal opportunities to study. A girl who does as (12) _____ as a boy knows that her chance to study further is as (13) _____ as (14) _____ . When they get their degrees, they (15) _____ for jobs fairly. So today, if you are a hardworking schoolgirl, you need not worry. You (16) _____ your career soon and you (17) _____ a chance to attain your ambition. This (18) _____ that you will be a (19) _____ housewife and mother. You (20) _____ able to handle both your career and your home.

1 A do not go		**8 A** clever	
B does not go		**B** more clever	
C did not go		**C** cleverer	
D did not went		**D** cleverest	
2 A learn		**9 A** she	
B learnt		**B** him	
C learning		**C** his	
D were learning		**D** he	
3 A a		**10 A** large, red	
B the		**B** large red	
C an		**C** red large	
D –		**D** red and large	
4 A preparing		**11 A** have	
B prepared		**B** are having	
C was preparing		**C** had	
D were preparing		**D** has	
5 A a		**12 A** good	
B an		**B** better	
C –		**C** best	
D the		**D** well	
6 A have		**13 A** better	
B has		**B** good	
C had		**C** well	
D were having		**D** best	
7 A less		**14 A** him	
B least		**B** he	
C little		**C** his	
D a little		**D** hers	

15 A will compete
   B will competing
   C competing
   D will competed

16 A will choosing
   B choosing
   C be choosing
   D will be choosing

17 A having
   B will having
   C will be having
   D will have

18 A does not means
   B do not mean
   C does not mean
   D do not means

19 A worse
   B bad
   C more worse
   D most bad

20 A will be
   B will
   C will being
   D being

D Rearrange the words to form correct sentences.

1 car — Dad's — dented — is — motorist — that — the — who.

_____

_____

2 because — came — heavy — home — Celia — late — of — rain — the.

_____

_____

3 but — can — cook — eat — he — John — out — prefers — to.

_____

_____

4 are — here — Larry — misplaced — notes — the — which.

_____

_____

5 decide — because — ended — late — meeting — much — there — the — was — so — to.

_____

_____

TEST 5

A Fill each blank with the most suitable word.

Chess is a game for two players. (1) _____ demands a lot of skill. Each player's aim
(2) _____ to trap his opponent's king. A player loses (3) _____ game when his king
cannot take a step (4) _____ any direction without being captured.

A chess set (5) _____ of a chequered board and 32 chess pieces. (6) _____ board
has 32 light squares and 32 dark (7) _____ . Sixteen of the chess pieces are also light
(8) _____ the other 16 are dark. The player who (9) _____ the light
pieces is called White. The player (10) _____ uses the dark pieces is called Black.

YOUR SCORE
10

B Read the passage below and answer the questions.

Mr and Mrs Lopez are shopkeepers. They own a grocery store and a stationery shop. Mr Lopez
runs the stationery shop and Mrs Lopez and their son Stanley run the grocery store beside it.

At 6 a.m. every morning, they leave their house in their van. They arrive at the shops about an
hour later. All three begin work immediately. Mr Lopez sweeps both shops and dusts the shelves.
Mrs Lopez sticks price tags on the new goods. Stanley carries boxes of things and arranges them on
the shelves.

By 8.30 a.m., all the work is finished and Mr and Mrs Lopez open their shops.

1 How many shops do Mr and Mrs Lopez own?

_____

_____

2 When do they leave their house in the morning?

_____

_____

3 Where do they go every morning?

_____

_____

4 How do they go there?

_____

_____

5 What does Stanley do before the shops open?

_____

YOUR SCORE
10

_____

$\boxed{C}$ Circle the letters of the correct answers to complete the passage below.

(1) _____ Sundays my family gets up (2) _____ unlike some other families. After breakfast, Mum (3) _____ the dishes, Dad (4) _____ them (5) _____ I place them (6) _____ the crockery cupboard. Then we tidy (7) _____ house, feed the cats, shower and (8) _____ off.

Sometimes we watch (9) _____ movie before lunch or (10) _____ a few hours at (11) _____ Park Lane where a flea market is held every Sunday. There (12) _____ many things to buy at the market. Mum loves (13) _____ for unusual teapots to add to (14) _____ collection. Dad and I (15) _____ to browse through old books. (16) _____ favourite stall is 'Joe's Gems' which (17) _____ books published as early as 1930.

At other times we may take a (18) _____ drive around the countryside or have lunch and tea at a (19) _____ restaurant overlooking the river. I look forward to Sundays (20) _____ it is a wonderful time for the family to be together.

1 A At
   B In
   C On
   D –

2 A early
   B earlier
   C earliest
   D the earliest

3 A wash
   B washes
   C washed
   D washing

4 A dry
   B dries
   C dried
   D is drying

5 A and
   B but
   C because
   D ,

6 A at
   B in
   C on
   D –

7 A a
   B an
   C the
   D –

8 A we
   B we're
   C they
   D they're

9 A a
   B an
   C the
   D –

10 A are spending
    B is spending
    C spent
    D spend

11 A a
    B an
    C the
    D –

12 A are
    B is
    C has
    D have

13	A	look		17	A	having
	B	looks			B	had
	C	is looking			C	has
	D	to look			D	have

14	A	she		18	A	slowest
	B	she's			B	slower
	C	hers			C	slowly
	D	her			D	slow

15	A	prefer		19	A	beauty
	B	prefers			B	beautiful
	C	preferred			C	more beautiful
	D	preferring			D	most beautiful

16	A	We		20	A	who
	B	Us			B	which
	C	Our			C	because
	D	Ours			D	and

YOUR SCORE
20

D Rearrange the words to form correct sentences.

1 Alan — because — canteen — fell — floor — in — slippery — the — the — was.

_____

_____

2 chased — handbag — Lily's — man — snatched — the — we — who.

_____

_____

3 because — cancelled — coach — he — ill — practice — tennis — the — our — was.

_____

_____

4 didn't — leopards — on — see — the — the — the — tree — were — which — zebra.

_____

_____

5 and — Ann — but — dancing — hates — her sister — it — like — their brother.

_____

_____

YOUR SCORE
10

TEST 6

A Fill each blank with the most suitable word.

Last year, we started preparing for our Teachers' Day celebrations by interviewing our teachers. Then (1) _____ wrote a very funny play and chose some (2) _____ to act as teachers. The students practised hard. (3) _____ acted very well on Teachers' Day. Everybody enjoyed (4) _____ play.

The teachers also entertained us. Some teachers (5) _____ were usually strict surprised us on that day. (6) _____ sang and danced for us.

Later, we played (7) _____ . We had basketball, badminton and table-tennis matches between (8) _____ and students. The teachers lost all the matches (9) _____ they were sporting. After that, we carried them (10) _____ our shoulders into the school hall for a grand lunch.

YOUR SCORE

10

B Read the passage and answer the questions on it.

Anita was at the river that morning to fetch a pail of water for her mother. At eight o'clock sharp, she heard the school bell ring. This made her sad because she could not go to school. Her parents just could not afford it.

Anita carried the heavy pail of water and walked onto the main road. Just then a car passed by. It stopped suddenly and a well-dressed man stepped out. He asked her how to get to the school and Anita gave him directions. As he was getting back into his car, his wallet fell out of his pocket but he did not notice. Anita quickly put down her pail and picked up the wallet. She handed it back to the man. He looked very pleased and asked Anita all about herself.

It turned out that the man was the new principal of the school. A month later, he visited Anita's parents and gave them the good news. Anita could attend school and she did not have to pay any fees.

1 Where was Anita that morning?

_____

_____

2 Why couldn't Anita go to school?

_____

_____

3 Who asked Anita for directions to the school?

_____

_____

4 What happened to the man's wallet?

_____

_____

5 When did the new principal of the school visit Anita's parents?

_____

_____

C Circle the letters of the correct answers to complete the passage below.

My dear Ray,

The letter (1) _____ you sent us a month ago arrived only yesterday. (2) _____ you get our address right next time, please? I know you (3) _____ a professor of physics (4) _____ professors are often forgetful (5) _____ surely you can remember your own family's address!

Just now I (6) _____ again at your letter. I noticed (7) _____ name in the return address and I (8) _____ even more amazed. May I (9) _____ you something? When did you (10) _____ your name from Raymond to Rayzone? You may (11) _____ deeply interested in ultraviolet rays and the ozone layer but your parents (12) _____ named you Raymond wouldn't really want a son called Rayzone.

I know you forget things because (13) _____ mind is on your work. Still, forgetting your own name is something (14) _____ is rather alarming. (15) _____ you are working a little too hard.

Mum and Dad are (16) _____ because Dad won two tickets to any destination (17) _____ the United States. They are going to visit you in Boston. They plan (18) _____ a month. They'd like to meet the girl who (19) _____ going to be their daughter-in-law one day.

Your family who will always forgive your forgetful ways sends you (20) _____ love and regards.

Your loving sister,
Rose

1 A who
  B which
  C where
  D when

2 A Maybe
  B May
  C Do
  D Can

3 A am
  B are
  C be
  D is

4 A and
  B but
  C who
  D which

5 A and
  B but
  C who
  D which

6 A look
  B looks
  C looked
  D looking

7	A	my	12	A	who	17	A	at
	B	mine		B	which		B	in
	C	your		C	are		C	on
	D	yours		D	were		D	–

8	A	am	13	A	you	18	A	stay
	B	is		B	you're		B	to stay
	C	was		C	your		C	stayed
	D	were		D	yours		D	will be staying

9	A	ask	14	A	and	19	A	am
	B	asks		B	but		B	are
	C	asked		C	who		C	be
	D	am asking		D	which		D	is

10	A	change	15	A	May	20	A	her
	B	changes		B	May be		B	my
	C	changed		C	Maybe		C	our
	D	changing		D	May think		D	their

11	A	am	16	A	excited
	B	is		B	exciting
	C	are		C	excites
	D	be		D	excite

YOUR SCORE 20

D Rearrange the words to form correct sentences.

1 and — five — for — have — I — papers — sit — to — you.

_____

2 am — aren't — I — I — rather — untidy,?

_____

3 brothers — is — man — my — that — the — tutors — who.

_____

_____

4 because — everyone — he — him — is — listens — to — sensible.

_____

_____

5 followed — led — quarry — the — the — they — to — trail — which.

_____

_____

YOUR SCORE 10

ANSWERS

1.1 ARTICLES

Practice A

1 an	**2** a	**3** an	**4** a	**5** an
6 an	**7** a	**8** a	**9** an	**10** a

Practice B

1 a	**2** An, a	**3** an
4 an, a	**5** a	**6** an, a, a

Practice C

2 crow, eagle
3 school, office
4 rose, orchid
5 sandwich, ice-cream
6 raincoat, umbrella

Practice D

2 Stella Jones is an accountant.
3 Eva Bonn is a singer.
4 Martin Chan is an optician.
5 Patrick Hill is an inspector.
6 Faizal Hussein is a lawyer.

Practice E

1 igloo, tent
2 adult, child
3 emerald, diamond
4 organ, ukelele
5 calculator, abacus

Practice F

1 Egyptian
2 house
3 orchard
4 owl
5 vet
6 Mexican
7 apartment
8 cinema
9 hamster
10 actor

Practice G

1 a burger
2 a plumber
3 an elevator
4 an operation
5 a U-turn

1.2 ARTICLES

Practice A

1 an, the	**2** the, the	**3** the, the
4 a, the	**5** an, The	

Practice B

1 a	**2** an	**3** a	**4** the	**5** a
6 the	**7** the	**8** a	**9** an	**10** the

Practice C

1 The sea is calm today.
2 Would you like an ice cube in your drink?
3 Lisa uses an apron when she cooks.
4 I have an orange and a pear. I'll keep the orange. Who wants the pear?
5 My father works in a bank. He leaves the house at 8.00 a.m. and arrives at the office at 8.30 a.m.

Practice D

1 a	**2** A	**3** the	**4** a	**5** a
6 an	**7** the	**8** the	**9** a	**10** the

Practice E

(line 4) the → a	(line 9) a → an
(line 5) A → The	(line 12) a → the
(line 6) a → an	(line 13) a → the
(line 7) a → the	(line 14) a → an
(line 8) the → a	(line 15) the → an

Practice F

An ant is an insect too. There are more than a million species of insects in the world. Insects have six legs. Their bodies are divided into three parts. The first part is the head. The second part is the thorax and the third part is the stomach.

Practice G

1 A, C	**2** A	**3** B, C	**4** A, B	**5** C	**6** B, C

1.3 ARTICLES

Practice A

1 the, –	**2** –, the	**3** –, The, the	**4** The, –, the

Practice B

The Mediterranean Sea is connected to the Atlantic Ocean by the Straits of ~~the~~ Gibraltar. It is connected to the Red Sea by the Suez ~~the~~ Canal. Long ago, traders on their way to ~~the~~ Europe or ~~the~~ Asia passed through the Mediterranean Sea. They also used some of the cities along the Mediterranean ~~the~~ coast as trading centres. Constantinople in ~~the~~ Turkey, ~~the~~ Venice in ~~the~~ Italy and ~~the~~ Barcelona in ~~the~~ Spain were important cities to them.

Practice C

1 the	**2** a	**3** the	**4** –	**5** the
6 –, the	**7** the	**8** an	**9** the	

Answers to the quiz:

1 in Africa
2 a single-wheeled cycle
3 Yuri Gagarin
4 in Argentina
5 in 1969
6 the Golden Gate bridge
7 Abraham Lincoln
8 a large flightless bird
9 5,584 km

Practice D

1 the	**2** –	**3** the	**4** –	**5** –
6 –	**7** the	**8** –	**9** the	**10** the

Practice E

1	3	5	6	9

Practice F
1 Indonesia
2 Hong Kong, the Tropic of Cancer
3 The Louvre, France
4 Somalia, the Indian Ocean
5 Maria Island, the Tasman Sea, Tasmania

Practice G

Gettysburg is **a** small town in Pennsylvania near **the** Susquehanna River. Gettysburg is famous in the history of **the** United States of America as **the** place where **an** important battle was fought during **the** American Civil War. **The** battle lasted from **the** 1st of July to **the** 3rd July 1863 and there were many casualties. The Union Army defeated **the** Confederate Army, but it was another two years before **the** Confederate Army surrendered. Abraham Lincoln gave **a** speech about democracy at Gettysburg and this speech is called **the** Gettysburg Address.

1.4 ARTICLES
Practice A

1 –, the	2 a, a	3 The, The
4 –, the, The	5 an, –	

Practice B

1 The	4 coffee, The coffee
2 a pinch of salt, salt	5 –, the
3 a cup of tea, tea, milk	

Practice C

1 an	2 The	3 –, –, –	4 a, a
5 an	6 The	7 –	

Practice D

1 Gold is /type of metal. [a]

2 Pewter is made by mixing tin with lead. [ ]

3 My brother has /pewter mug. [a]

4 /Bronze lamp in my sitting room is from India. [The]

5 Bronze is / alloy of copper and tin. [an]

Practice E

1 Tennis, game	2 ribbon, lace	3 drop, blood
4 lump, clay	5 item, clothing	

Practice F
2 Peter doesn't eat meat. He is a vegetarian.
4 Where is the tube of glue I bought yesterday?
5 I prefer golf to squash.

Practice G
2 a petrol station
3 the petrol station
4 petrol / a can of petrol
5 the petrol station
6 a petrol attendant / the petrol attendant
7 a container
8 the container / the petrol
9 the container / the bottom of the container
10 the petrol
11 The petrol attendant

2 POSSESSIVES
Practice A
1 A giraffe's neck is very long.
2 The boys' parents took them on holiday.

3 Anna's mother is a lawyer.
4 The girls' voices are excellent.
5 She drew four elephant and painted the elephants' trunks brown.
6 Peter took his dogs to the vet. The vet checked the dogs' ears.
7 Rachel borrowed Jan's dictionary yesterday.
8 I bought a dress from the ladies' department.
9 The businessmen's meeting is at the Orchid Hotel.
10 The pony's owner rode it round the field.

Practice B
2 Jill's essay is about her childhood.
3 The writer of the book is Alice King.
4 The heels of my shoes are broken.

Practice C
2 Liz is Tony's wife.
3 Roger and Liz are Tim's children.
4 Rose is Ben's sister.
5 Ricky and Mike are Winnie's sons / children.
6 Ben is Ricky's cousin.

Practice D
1 Eric's grandparents
2 aunts' favourite hobby
3 David's pet
4 the basement of the house
5 women's magazines
6 The students' laughter
7 My classmate's sister
8 the bars of the cage
9 policewomen's uniforms
10 the funny parts of the movie

Practice E

2 dogs'	7 neighbours'
3 ladies'	8 the window of the room
4 smell of smoke	9 the Samsons'
5 ladies' kitchen	10 Mr Gopal's
6 fireman's	11 the ladies' best friends

3.1 PERSONAL PRONOUNS AS SUBJECTS
Practice A

1 They	2 We	3 You	4 She	5 It
6 It	7 She	8 They	9 He	10 They

Practice B

1 They, he	2 He, They	3 I, we
4 She, it	5 I, he	

Practice C

1 It	2 He	3 They	4 She	5 She
6 We	7 He	8 They	9 It	10 They

Practice D

1 we	2 They	3 She	4 He	5 You
6 They	7 It	8 They	9 It	10 She

Practice E
2 Billy looked after all the animals in the pet zoo. He said they loved visitors.
3 You and Anne look unwell. You should see Dr Carlos. He/She is good.
4 Grandpa is talkative but Grandma is quiet. He says she doesn't get a chance to talk.
5 One of the postmen in my hometown was excellent. He looked at envelopes with names but no addresses and knew where they should go.
6 You and I should take up gymnastics. It will be fun and

we will get a lot of good exercise.

Practice F

2	I	3	We	4	She	5	They	6	He
7	you	8	We	9	I	10	She	11	It

3.2 PERSONAL PRONOUNS AS SUBJECTS AND OBJECTS

Practice A

1	her	2	it	3	you	4	us	5	them
6	him	7	me	8	them	9	it	10	her

Practice B

1	her	2	He, us	3	She	4	me, It
5	They	6	I, it	7	It		

Practice C

1	She	2	We	3	me, you	4	them, It
5	he, her	6	We, us				

Practice D

2	B, C	3	A, B	4	A, C	5	A, B	6	B, C

Practice E

2	I	3	he	4	him	5	she	6	her
7	me	8	us	9	it	10	they	11	We

3.3 POSSESSIVE PRONOUNS AND POSSESSIVE ADJECTIVES

Practice A

1	B	2	A	3	A	4	B	5	B
6	B	7	B	8	A	9	B	10	A

Practice B

1	Your	2	My	3	it	4	its	5	my
6	your	7	Our	8	their	9	our	10	us

Practice C

2	our, theirs	3	his, her	4	her, ours		
5	his, yours	6	their, mine				

Practice D

2	my	3	yours	4	his	5	my	6	Its
7	their	8	theirs	9	our	10	Your	11	my

Practice E

2 The scouts put up their tents near ours.
3 After finishing her meal, she gives the hamster its food.
4 His son's face is exactly like his.
5 I'll wear this dress for my first party because I like its colour.
6 The small room is yours and the big one is theirs.

Practice F

2	their	3	theirs	4	its	5	his	6	her
7	my	8	mine	9	our	10	his	11	hers

3.4 DEMONSTRATIVE PRONOUNS AND DEMONSTRATIVE ADJECTIVES

Practice A

1	Those	4	These	6	this, that
2	This	5	These, Those	7	these, those
3	That				

Practice B

2 Those hens are fat.   5 That is a beautiful hornbill.
3 These apples are sweet. 6 That building is modern.
4 This is a heavy book.

Practice C

2 These are jugglers.   5 That is an acrobat.

3 This is a clown.   6 That is the lion.
4 This is the lion trainer.

Practice D

2	That	3	that	4	these	5	those	6	Those
7	These	8	this	9	this	10	This	11	those

Practice E

3 All this furniture here must be dusted.
5 This pair of shoes is more stylish than the others.
6 Look at that out there in the field!

Practice F

1	This	2	those	3	this	4	this	5	those
6	this	7	these	8	those	9	those	10	that

4 GENDER

Practice A

1	She, it	2	He, them	3	gorilla, elephant
4	He, it	5	He, her		

Practice B

bachelor	doe	hero	hostess	gentleman
mare	nun	peacock	ram	stewardess

Practice C

Masculine		Feminine	
1	bachelor	1	doe
2	hero	2	hostess
3	gentleman	3	mare
4	peacock	4	nun
5	ram	5	stewardess

Practice D

1	He	2	It	3	her	4	They	5	It
6	them	7	him	8	his	9	hers	10	him

Practice E

1	Miss Chang	6	nephew
2	My brother	7	mother-in-law
3	lioness	8	head boy
4	My father	9	princess
5	His	10	salesgirl

Practice F

1	my aunt	6	her fiancé
2	the waiter	7	the actor's
3	the policewoman	8	the empress
4	the bridegroom	9	the widow
5	the witch's	10	the landlord

Practice G

1	sister	5	man	8	nephews
2	girl	6	them	9	it
3	brothers	7	niece	10	him
4	husband				

Practice H

1	sisters	5	woman	8	mother
2	It	6	husband	9	her
3	its	7	boys	10	it
4	landlady				

5.1 ADJECTIVES

Practice A

2 small purple van
3 black and orange / orange and black handbag
4 tiny blue stones
5 huge brown animal
6 green and white / white and green house

7 large grey umbrella
8 black and green / green and black
9 huge purple mask
10 red and white / white and red
11 small brown cupboard

Practice B
4 I like those orange ∧ grey cushions.

5 Stephanie bought a brown ∧ black belt.

7 We saw a yellow ∧ black snake at the zoo.

9 The grey ∧ white building belongs to our company.

11 Let's buy this orange ∧ brown wrapping paper.

Practice C
1 A   2 A, B, C   3 B   4 B, C   5 C   6 A, B

Practice D
1 luxurious
2 long red body
3 black
4 tiny golden
5 spacious
6 grey and brown
7 shiny
8 extra
9 slim silver
10 sophisticated

Practice E
2 Sam drives a small truck.
3 My balloon is pink and blue / blue and pink.
4 These apples are big. / These are big apples.
5 I have a red and green / green and red pencil box.
6 Mary's earrings are huge.

Practice F
2 This ring is expensive.
3 Joe's TV set is large.
4 That insect is tiny.
5 Michael's baseball cap is red and black.
6 The fish in this pond are small.

5.2 ADJECTIVES OF COMPARISON
Practice A
2 more talkative
3 most dangerous
4 finer
5 tastiest
6 stronger
7 more difficult
8 thinner
9 thickest
10 most popular
11 earlier

Practice B
2 Julie is the tidiest of the sisters.
3 I have more interesting games than Chris.
4 Hillary is the most hardworking among us.
5 Your aquarium is more expensive than mine.
6 Mark is the friendliest man in my neighbourhood.

Practice C
1 cheaper, the cheapest
2 more luxurious, the most luxurious
3 nearer, the nearest
4 more peaceful, the most peaceful
5 more interesting, the most interesting

Practice D
2 Maggie is more elegant than Beth.
3 Beth is younger than Maggie.
4 Maggie is taller than Beth.
5 Beth is more cheerful than Maggie.
6 Maggie is neater than Beth.

Practice E
1 the fastest
2 faster than
6 tastier than
7 more delicious than

3 the busiest
4 the most terrible
5 the best
8 more efficient than
9 kinder than
10 the most understanding

6 ADVERBS
Practice A
better   early   excitedly   hard   kindly
quietly   strangely   tenderly   tightly   warmly

Practice B
1 hungrily
2 heavily
3 far
4 loudly
5 alone
6 long
7 silently
8 frequently
9 straight
10 late

Practice C
1 Kelly ∧ carried the box ∧ from the car ∧.

2 Lola practises ∧ to be a gymnast.

3 The lions growled ∧ at us ∧.

4 The Italian team ∧ won the motorcycle rally ∧.

5 He ∧ carved the piece of wood ∧.

Practice D
1 patiently
2 skilfully
3 deep
4 happily
5 hard
6 carefully
7 quietly
8 fierce
9 loosely
10 quickly

Practice E
1 A   2 B   3 A   4 A   5 B

Practice F
2 lovingly
3 beautifully
4 richly
5 perfectly
6 accurately
7 usually
8 fast
9 well
10 straight
11 completely

Practice G
1 lately → late
2 highly → high
3 proudly → proud
4 lowly → low
5 good → well

7.1 SUBJECT-VERB AGREEMENT
Practice A
2 Doctors take care of patients.
3 Birds have feathers.
4 The soldiers are brave.
5 The children laugh happily.
6 They play netball very well.

Practice B
2 washes
3 are
4 am
5 enjoy
6 studies
7 is
8 give
9 is
10 saves
11 go

Practice C
1 are, have
4 is, looks
2 do, prefer
5 follow, graze
3 is, makes

Practice D
1 were cheering
2 is
3 are
4 are moving
5 reveal
6 is
7 damages
8 touches
9 prefer
10 has got

Practice E

1	takes	5	writes	8	rise
2	hold	6	was	9	cultivates
3	is	7	is grazing	10	is
4	has				

Practice F

It has a large tea plantation. The cool climate here is suitable for tea-growing. Many people in the town work as tea pickers. They pick the young tea leaves and put them in baskets. Then they carry these baskets of tea leaves to the factory for processing.

7.2 SUBJECT-VERB AGREEMENT

Practice A

2 do not / don't exercise in the morning.
3 is not / isn't at home.
4 are not / aren't artists.
5 does not / doesn't have a long tail.
6 do not / don't have blue eyes.

Practice B

2 Kim does not / doesn't want an ice-cream.
3 Amy does not / doesn't own a bicycle.
4 My cat does not / doesn't eat mice.
5 She is not / isn't the best actress in the movie.
6 We are not / aren't in the school team.

Practice C

1 We do not live in town.
2 Our houses are not near the highway.
3 Our farm is not big.
4 The village does not have a cinema.
5 We do not see many tourists in our area.

Practice D

2 Japan is not / isn't a city.
3 Lily does not / doesn't have an aquarium.
4 My mother does not / doesn't speak Mandarin.
5 Mercury is not / isn't a gas.
6 A rhino does not / doesn't have a hump.

Practice E

1 ain't → am not   4 isn't → doesn't
2 wants → want   5 doesn't → don't
3 thinks → think

Practice F

1 She isn't want to be late for work. → She doesn't / does not want to be late for work.
2 In the office she not waste time. → In the office she doesn't / does not waste time.
3 Laura's colleagues isn't as hardworking as she is. → Laura's colleagues aren't / are not as hardworking as she is.
4 Most of them doesn't think she is doing the right thing. → Most of them don't / do not think she is doing the right thing.
5 They think it aren't wise of her to work such long hours. → They think it isn't / is not wise of her to work such long hours.

7.3 SUBJECT-VERB AGREEMENT

Practice A

2 Does she wear contact lenses?
3 Is Australia near New Zealand?

4 Do giant pandas eat bamboo leaves?
5 Are the campers safe from wild animals?
6 Do many tourists visit this cheesecake factory?

Practice B

1 Are	2 Do	3 Is	4 Do	5 Is
6 Do	7 Is	8 Do	9 Is	10 Do

Practice C

1 Do, want   2 Is   3 Do, like   4 Are
5 Do, prefer   6 Are   7 Is

Practice D

2 Is Fiona a dentist?
3 Do their sons clean the house? / Do the sons clean their house?
4 Are the boys at the gymnasium?
5 Is your furniture new?
6 Does Mr Hobbs fetch his daughters on Wednesdays?

Practice E

1 Is → Are   4 Are → Is
2 spent → spend   5 has → have
3 wants → want

Practice F

1	Is	5	Is	8	Do, sell
2	Do, know	6	Are	9	Is
3	Are	7	Do, have	10	Do, want
4	Does, serve				

8.1 PRESENT TENSE

Practice A

1	is calling	5	is buying	8	cycles
2	is teaching	6	are studying	9	exercises
3	hunt	7	wake up	10	is preparing
4	read				

Practice B

1 sews, is sewing   4 jog, are jogging
2 is delivering, delivers   5 takes, is taking
3 eat, is eating

Practice C

2	begin	6	talk	9	is
3	is leaving	7	patrols	10	plays
4	is arriving	8	are making	11	end
5	attends				

Practice D

1	love	5	is snowing	8	put
2	writes	6	breathe	9	have
3	is resting	7	plays	10	are weaving
4	hurries				

Practice E

2	requires	6	likes	10	takes
3	leaves	7	is demonstrating	11	presents
4	helps	8	is acting		
5	enjoys	9	are watching / watch		

Practice F

1	have	5	want	8	are following
2	is watching	6	am	9	start
3	are waiting	7	are playing	10	insists
4	prefer				

8.2 SIMPLE PAST TENSE

Practice A

2	were	5	stand	8	appear	10	stretch
3	laid	6	stare	9	raise	11	seem
4	come	7	feel				

Practice B

2	fried	5	collected	8	fed	10	took
3	made	6	put	9	swept	11	cleaned
4	helped	7	left				

Practice C

2	dry	5	bakes	8	were	10	hurt
3	woke	6	have	9	arrived	11	revises
4	stole	7	played				

Practice D

2	made	5	led	8	hurried	10	prevented
3	peeped	6	guessed	9	removed	11	came
4	saw	7	called				

Practice E

1 is bathing
2 found
3 cost
4 brought
5 does / did
6 thinks / thought
7 let
8 burnt
9 scolded
10 go

Practice F

2	accompanies	6	realised	9	ran
3	remained	7	felt	10	flung
4	had	8	headed	11	came
5	set				

8.3 PAST CONTINUOUS TENSE

Practice A

1   4   5   7   9

Practice B

1 grow
2 is writing
3 am studying
4 was repairing
5 was talking
6 were enjoying
7 fell
8 is hurrying
9 feeds
10 are climbing

Practice C

1 was reading
2 rushed
3 was clutching
4 shone
5 pointed
6 stared
7 was talking
8 found
9 leapt
10 threw

Practice D

1 stood / was standing
2 makes
3 runs / is running
4 are searching
5 was pruning
6 spread
7 was tapping / tapped
8 lent
9 is spraying
10 destroyed

Practice E

2	heard	6	was heading	9	swung
3	was	7	shouted	10	crashed
4	was speeding	8	noticed	11	fell
5	was trying				

8.4 SIMPLE FUTURE TENSE

Practice A

1	sees	4	need	7	cutting	9	faced
2	begin	5	will	8	was	10	vanish
3	increase	6	produce				

Practice B

The school bus will pick him up in the morning and his father will fetch him home in his car in the afternoon. In school, he will listen to his teacher carefully and will do all his work in class. He will ask his teacher some questions. At home, his elder brother will help him with his homework.

James will play games in school with his friends. They will do many other things together. They will be happy. They will help one another. They will enjoy their time at school.

Practice C

1 is going to
2 will visit
3 are going to
4 will apply
5 will hold
6 will be
7 move
8 will take
9 enter
10 are going to

Practice D

1 I will sit for my final exam this November.
2 Our football team will be in Madrid next week.
3 Linda will become the head prefect next year.
4 Our Science Club will visit that chocolate factory next Friday.
5 My neighbour is going to renovate his house.

Practice E

1 joined
2 rose
3 employed
4 got
5 holds
6 gave
7 will, be
8 will celebrate / are going to celebrate
9 will compere / are going to compere
10 will present / are going to present

Practice F

1 will be / am going to be
2 fell
3 will direct / is going to direct
4 will return
5 am
6 spent
7 sounds
8 lived
9 was
10 had

8.5 FUTURE CONTINUOUS TENSE

Practice A

1 will arrive
2 is skating
3 will be holding
4 are fishing
5 will be taking
6 listens
7 sweeps
8 are swimming
9 will be moving
10 found

Practice B

1 leaving
2 helped
3 is mowing
4 flying
5 borrowed
6 takes
7 am cleaning
8 calling
9 is bathing
10 will be

Practice C

2 will be drawing up, will be contacting
3 will be cleaning, will be decorating
4 will be putting up, will be arranging
5 will be assembling, will be testing
6 will be writing, will be delivering

Practice D

1 will be ending
2 are
6 are
7 know

3 are going to do
4 will be
5 hopes

8 will be studying
9 will choose
10 have

Practice E
1 will be celebrating
2 will enjoy
3 will be buying
4 will mean
5 will be

6 will be giving
7 are
8 will be driving
9 promised
10 will definitely change

Practice F
1 lives
2 joined
3 learnt
4 is
5 will be sending

6 will be attending
7 returns
8 will make
9 will be going
10 plans

9 SUBJECT AND PREDICATE
Practice A
3 Tokyo ∧ a large city.

5 I ∧ from the United States.

6 You ∧ pretty in that dress.

9 Paul ∧ at the station on time.

10 Larry ∧ here just now.

Practice B
1 We bought the watermelons at a supermarket.
2 Our neighbour is friendly.
3 Hans likes spicy food.
4 She finished her work fast.
5 He was the manager there.

Practice C
1   2   4   5   7

Practice D
2 Chris is a good manager.
3 Some camels have two humps.
4 You can phone your mother now.
5 The weather was fine yesterday.
6 My neighbour makes porridge for breakfast.

Practice E
2 A, B, C   **3** A, C   **4** B, C   **5** A, B   **6** C

Practice F
2 He draws in his room at night excellent cartoons. → He draws excellent cartoons in his room at night.

3 Their funny behaviour and words he notices. → He notices their funny behaviour and words.

4 Makes them even funnier than they are. → He makes them even funnier than they are.

5 She said, "You a lot of talent." → She said, "You have a lot of talent."

6 The teacher is sure that Ian will be in his country one of the best cartoonists. → The teacher is sure that Ian will be one of the best cartoonists in his country.

10 FINITE AND NON-FINITE VERBS
Practice A
2 heard
3 had
4 are
5 have

7 am waiting
8 was
9 are
10 is trying

6 did

11 am

Practice B
1 B   **2** A   **3** A   **4** B   **5** A

Practice C
1 were
2 have to repair
3 was
4 to cycle
5 failed

6 knocked
7 will take care
8 riding
9 gives
10 repair

Practice D
1 The students are to go to the stadium now.
2 The factory workers have to be ready for a fire drill.
3 The goose is chasing the thief.
4 Susie wants to learn Japanese next year.
5 Our music teacher is training the choir for our concert.

Practice E
2 to be → have to be

3 running → was running

4 decide → decided

5 not dividing → am not dividing

6 to report → are to report

Practice F
2 flowed
3 loved
4 played

5 make
6 have
7 had

8 is
9 flow

10 am
11 are

11 QUESTION TAGS
Practice A
1 isn't she
2 aren't they
3 isn't it
4 aren't we

5 aren't I
6 aren't they
7 aren't we

8 isn't he
9 aren't you
10 isn't it

Practice B
1 isn't it
2 aren't I
3 aren't they
4 aren't we

5 isn't it
6 isn't she
7 aren't you

8 isn't he
9 aren't they
10 isn't it

Practice C
4   6   5   3   2

Practice D
1 isn't it
2 aren't they
3 isn't she
4 aren't you

5 aren't they
6 aren't I
7 isn't it

8 isn't it
9 aren't you
10 aren't I

Practice E
2 B, C   **3** B, C   **4** A, C   **5** A, B   **6** A, C

Practice F
3 am I? → aren't I?

4 aren't they? → isn't she?

6 aren't they? → isn't he?

8 aren't they? → isn't it?

9 are not we? → aren't we?

12.1 WH-QUESTIONS
Practice A
2   3   6   9   10

Practice B
1 Where was he
2 How do you make
3 Why were you

4 When do they want
5 Which student has

Practice C

2 B   3 B   4 A   5 B   6 A

Practice D

1 did, leave
2 are you, hanging
3 do, finish
4 does Jenny, make
5 When are your cousins, returning

Practice E

1 ⟨Who⟩ in the meeting room?

2 What ⟨the matter⟩ with Hannah?

3 Why ⟨Kathy and Jim⟩ so upset last night?

4 Which ⟨college⟩ your brothers in?

5 ⟨When⟩ Sports Day last year?

6 How far ⟨Kyoto⟩ from Tokyo?

7 How much pepper ⟨there⟩ in this packet?

8 Whose ⟨design⟩ the most colourful?

9 Where ⟨my earrings⟩?

10 How many ⟨students⟩ absent yesterday?

Practice F

2 Which is Edward's parcel?
3 Who was she talking to just now?
4 When do you appear on television?
5 What do those restaurants serve for breakfast?
6 How many members does the Drama Society have?

Practice G

2 Which book does Robert want?
3 Who is in charge of this games stall?
4 When are you taking the driving test?
5 Whose house did the thieves break into?
6 Why are / were the workers running out of the factory?

12.2 WH-QUESTIONS

Practice A

1   4   5   7   9

Practice B

2 Who sent these flowers?
3 Who are those people?
4 Who is baking a cake?
5 Who was the goalkeeper?
6 Who wants a glass of water?

Practice C

2 Who went to the library with Mike?
3 Who is looking after the children?
4 Who was on the phone just now?
5 Who goes to school by bus?
6 Who are / is in charge of the project?

Practice D

1 Who is fetching you from the office?
2 Who likes photography?
3 Who made this meat pie?
4 Who has my postcards?
5 Who is with your grandmother now?

Practice E

1 needs
2 has
3 are
4 gave
5 is
6 expects
7 was
8 going
9 took
10 hoping

Practice F

2 Who are your favourite actors?
3 Who were the men in front of your house last night?
4 Who cooks the meals in your family?
5 Who plays the violin in your class?
6 Who attends tuition classes in your neighbourhood?

12.3 WH-QUESTIONS

Practice A

1 What
2 What
3 Who
4 What
5 Who
6 Who
7 What
8 What
9 Who
10 Who

Practice B

2 What are you eating?
3 What size is your shirt?
4 What is the baby holding?
5 What did the postman deliver just now?
6 What do they keep in that little cupboard?

Practice C

1 A, C   2 A   3 B   4 C
5 B   6 A, C   7 B   8 C

Practice D

1 A: What is   B: What does
2 A: Who made   B: What did
3 A: Who is   B: What are
4 A: What does   B: Who wants
5 A: What is   B: Who agrees

Practice E

2 What is the best-selling item in this shop?
3 What type of songs does Ken Rogers sing?
4 Who are you voting for as the chairman of our society?
5 What exercises are useful for strengthening the spine?
6 What paint are you using for the walls of your room?

Practice F

2 What is the name of the restaurant?
3 What food does it serve?
4 What time does it open?
5 What makes it popular with the office crowd?
6 What is Mr Lee planning to introduce at the restaurant next year?

12.4 WH-QUESTIONS

Practice A

2 My neighbour is Mr Graham. / Mr Graham is my neighbour.
3 Who has many dogs?
4 Who is staying with her?
5 A branch fell on my car.
6 What were they carrying just now?

Practice B

1 Mrs Reed is playing with the cats.
2 A dog is under the table.
3 Kim and Lynn are at the door.
4 They are holding racquets/tennis racquets.
5 Her hobby is reading.

Practice C

2 They are anteaters.

3 My favourite book is 'My Family and Other Animals'.
4 Maurice made it. / that unusual box.
5 My cousin was with me just now.
6 Some eggs are in that basket.

Practice D
1 B   2 A   3 C   4 B   5 C

Practice E
2 Children read her books.
3 They were mainly about animals.
4 Beatrix Potter wrote 'The Tale of Peter Rabbit'.
5 It was 'The Tailor of Gloucester.'
6 She illustrated her own stories.

12.5 WH-QUESTIONS
Practice A
1 C   2 C   3 B   4 A   5 A

Practice B
2 liked
3 Your rabbit, does eat
4 James and John, looks, his
5 Steve, did find
6 Gina, visited

Practice C
1 does, wants   2 does, does   3 have, had
4 What, I   5 likes, like

Practice D
1 I wish to invite Alice and her brother for our party.
2 She wants a packet of tea.
3 He plans to make a wooden table this weekend.
4 He hopes to meet his old friend Mr Khoo in Beijing.
5 We usually give her / our mother flowers on her birthday.

Practice E
1 She studied fashion design (in Hong Kong).
2 She met a talent scout / Richard Woods during one of the fashion shows.
3 He asked her to go for a screen test.
4 She acted as the owner of a fashion house in her first movie.
5 She wants to be a film director five years from now.

Practice F
3 What did Larry ask the hotel clerk for?
4 Who did Larry ask for directions to the post office?
5 Who did the hotel clerk give a map to?
6 What did the hotel clerk give Larry?
7 What did Larry accidentally put into the letterbox?

12.6 WH-QUESTIONS
Practice A
1 Who   2 What   3 Where   4 Where   5 When
6 What   7 Who   8 When   9 What   10 Where

Practice B
1 Where, When   2 When, Where   3 Where, When
4 Where, When   5 When, Where

Practice C
2 When did   3 He left   4 When is
5 Where will   6 I / We want

Practice D
2 Where will you be tomorrow?
3 When will the train arrive?
4 When will you telephone me?

5 Where are the suitcases?
6 When are the guests coming?

Practice E
2 He broke six world records in 45 minutes at Ann Arbor, Michigan.
3 It was in 1936.
4 He won four gold medals at the Berlin Olympics.
5 Hitler was angry at Owens' success.
6 Another athlete broke Owens' world record for the long jump in 1960.

Practice F
4 What does Kim study at the language centre every Friday?
5 Where does Kim study French every Friday?
6 When does Kim study French at the language centre?
7 Where will he meet Janet and Kim this afternoon?
8 When will he meet Janet and Kim at the Louvre?

12.7 WH-QUESTIONS
Practice A
1 When   4 Who   7 Which   9 Which
2 Whose   5 What   8 Whose   10 Whose
3 Which   6 Where

Practice B
1 are   4 do   7 barks   9 restaurants
2 vote   5 work   8 like   10 was
3 this   6 essay

Practice C
2   3   6   7   9

Practice D
2 Which singer won the competition?
3 Whose slippers are in the corner?
4 Whose raincoat did you borrow?
5 Which student hurt himself just now?
6 Which ones do you like?

Practice E
1 Mr Norton's son is an excellent artist.
2 He attended the Disney Art School.
3 'Miracle at Midnight' won the Grand Prize.
4 Philip Dempster's art gallery wants to buy 'Miracle at Midnight'.
5 I entered the 'Artists of the World' art competition.

Practice F
1 Vijaya Lakshmi Pandit's brother was the first Prime Minister of India.
2 Indira Gandhi served as Prime Minister of India twice.
3 Jawarharlal Nehru's sister was the first female president of the General Assembly of the United Nations.
4 Indira Gandhi's son died in a plane crash.
5 Rajiv Gandhi was killed by a bomb in 1991.

12.8 WH-QUESTIONS
Practice A
1   3   8   9   10

Practice B
1 How old is your grandmother?
2 She is eighty years old.
3 How many grandchildren does she have?
4 She has five grandchildren.
5 How much time do they spend with her?

Practice C

1 How far is your home from your office?
2 How many pairs of shoes do you have?
3 How much sugar is there in the container?
4 How expensive is that antique urn?
5 How many jars of jam did you want?

Practice D

2 How many computers did Mr Gan buy for his office?
3 How old is the museum?
4 How much money do you have?
5 How many students are absent today?
6 How much flour does Sara want?

Practice E

1 Twenty men searched for Jamie.
2 He was five years old.
3 They had four children.
4 It took them two hours (to find Jamie).
5 He made two railings.

Practice F

2 Who realised (that) Jamie was not around?
3 When did Cilla last see Jamie?
4 Where was Jamie when Nikko spotted him?
5 How much milk was there in the bottle?
6 Which doors did Mr Kent make railings for?

12.9 WH-QUESTIONS

Practice A

2 do → are

3 does → do

4 Jenny is → is Jenny

5 goes → go

6 the students were → were the students

Practice B

1 Whose
2 Why
3 How much
4 Where
5 How tall
6 Why
7 When
8 Whose
9 Why
10 Why

Practice C

1 was, staring
2 did, call
3 is, climbing
4 do, eat
5 were, shouting
6 does
7 did, write
8 is
9 are
10 is, running

Practice D

2 Why are they unhappy now?
3 Why are / were you banging on the door?
4 Why did he work with Mary this morning?
5 Why did Mr Ingram take the bus to work yesterday?
6 Why were you limping just now?

Practice E

1 Why was he shouting?
2 It took my cap.
3 Why are you sleepy?
4 I spilt orange juice on it.
5 Why does Ron visit you every evening?

Practice F

1 She wants to stay in her room because she coloured her hair and she thinks she looks awful.
2 She chose orange for her hair because she thought it would match her orange dress for the party.

3 She is miserable because she is not going to the party.
4 She won't go to the party because she is afraid Rachel and the others will laugh at her.
5 Mum says that Sue should not wear the orange dress because it is not suitable if she is going to the party as a clown.

13 MODALS

Practice A

1 B   2 A   3 C   4 A   5 B

Practice B

1   3   4   6   7

Practice C

2 May I have your address?
3 That flower may be an orchid.
4 Can I take one of these leaflets?
5 Can you play the guitar?
6 You may borrow my bicycle.

Practice D

2 Can you
3 Can I / May I
4 Can I / May I
5 Can I / May I
6 may be
7 You can / You may
8 can
9 may
10 can
11 may be

Practice E

2 can
3 may
4 can
5 may
6 can
7 can
8 can
9 may
10 can
11 can

Practice F

2 I can show your letter and pictures to a magazine editor here? → Can I / May I show your letter and pictures to a magazine editor here?
3 You maybe the person she is looking for. → You may be the person she is looking for.
4 I'm sure you'll say that I may asked you anything. → I'm sure you'll say that I can / I may ask you anything.
5 I want to know if can I be a successful artist one day. → I want to know if I can be a successful artist one day.
6 I may trying another career. → I may try another career.

14.1 PREPOSITIONS OF POSITION

Practice A

1 at, in
2 on, beside
3 at, on
4 in, on
5 in, beside

Practice B

2 the clothes line
3 the road
4 the top shelf of that cupboard
5 the restaurant
6 a lake

Practice C

1   2   3   7   9

Practice D

2 on
3 beside
4 at
5 on
6 on
7 beside
8 on
9 at
10 in
11 on

Practice E

1 on
2 in
3 at
4 on
5 in
6 beside
7 in
8 in / on
9 on
10 on

14.2 PREPOSITIONS OF TIME

Practice A

1 on	**2** at	**3** in	**4** on	**5** at
6 in	**7** in	**8** on	**9** on	**10** at

Practice B

2 Sunday morning

3 one summer

4 May

5 9 p.m.

6 each evening

Practice C

2 July, the afternoon

3 midnight, 11 p.m.

4 at breakfast, at 7 a.m., in the morning

5 last Sunday, on Sunday, in May

Practice D

1 I saw the mysterious figure one evening.

2 Our new house will be ready in April.

3 Sean and his friends play basketball every weekend.

4 Mrs Stevens was in Colombo for a conference last month.

5 I have many clothes to iron each day.

Practice E

2 I woke up suddenly at midnight.

3 The police arrested the kidnappers on 21st May.

4 Janet stays at home on Christmas Day.

5 Richard intends to resign from the company next month.

6 The ship sent out distress signals in the evening.

Practice F

1 at	**2** on	**3** –	**4** in	**5** at
6 in	**7** in	**8** at	**9** –	**10** on

15 PUNCTUATION

Practice A

1 4 6 7 9

Practice B

1 That boy , kite.

2 Look out! , you!

3 Where's , box?

4 aren't , They're

5 holiday's , mustn't

Practice C

2 Where's the letter?

3 He doesn't know how to boil an egg.

4 Oh dear! I can't find my bus ticket!

5 Don't worry. I won't lose the money.

6 The documents aren't with me. They're with Christine.

Practice D

2 They're	5 time.	8 tank?	10 dolphin's
3 don't	6 That's	9 isn't	11 snout!
4 We	7 man's		

Practice E

2 Those boys aren't interested in football.

3 James couldn't find his way to your house.

4 Mum, Aunt Mary's on the phone.

5 We're excited about the trip to Tasmania.

6 Mr Norton won't be attending the meeting.

Practice F

(line 2)	upstairs?	(line 7)	can't
(line 3)	doing.	(line 8)	Please
(line 4)	I'm	(line 9)	now.
(line 5)	goodness!	(line 10)	Dinner's
(line 6)	You've	(line 11)	doesn't

16.1 SENTENCE STRUCTURE

Practice A

1 but	5 and	8 and
2 and	6 drawing	9 hardworking
3 could not come	7 likes	10 small
4 but		

Practice B

1 A	2 B	3 B	4 A	5 C

Practice C

1 and, but	2 but, and	3 and, but
4 but, and	5 and, but	

Practice D

1 Cats are tame animals but tigers are wild animals.

2 He cooked a new dish but nobody ate it.

3 She shouted for help and a passerby stopped to help her.

4 The boys went to the movies and the girls went shopping.

5 Sally searched everywhere for her bracelet but she could not find it.

Practice E

2 5 6 8 10

Practice F

2 but	6 exciting	9 but
3 am not	7 and	10 miss
4 experienced	8 good	11 and
5 full		

16.2 SENTENCE STRUCTURE

Practice A

1 C	2 A	3 B	4 B	5 C

Practice B

1 , and	4 and but
2 but and	5 , and
3 , ,	

Practice C

1 C, A	2 C, A, B	3 C, C, A	4 A, B / B, A

Practice D

1 Elaine cut the vegetables, I washed them and Elizabeth cooked them.

2 The bus crashed into a tree and the driver was injured but the passengers escaped unhurt.

3 I bought the cake, Amy chose the present and Sam made the birthday card for Mum.

4 This is Sue's sculpture, that is Larry's oil painting and those are my textile designs.

5 My dad is good at carpentry but my brother isn't good at it and I'm not good at it either.

Practice E

1 and	2 but	3 ,	4 ,	5 and
6 but	7 and	8 ,	9 and	10 but

Practice F

1 I am quite good at squash but he is more practised and he is stronger.

2 The engine is coughing, the doors are rattling but the car is still running.

3 The story is exciting, the stars are attractive and their acting is good.

4 Cats and dogs usually fight but your cat and my dog are good friends and I love to watch them play together.

5 The curry was too hot, the vegetables were too salty and the rice was too soft.

16.3 SENTENCE STRUCTURE

Practice A
1 who love spicy curries
2 who is on duty today
3 who is very conscientious
4 who are both very artistic
5 who won the oratorical contest
6 who was trying to break into the office
7 who gave me some tablets for my headache
8 who recommended you for the job
9 who always drops in for a chat
10 who can advise him about his studies

Practice B

1	is	6	has
2	who	7	dentists
3	who	8	who loves
4	workers	9	are
5	makes	10	boy

Practice C
1   5   6   8   10

Practice D
1 who owns a boutique.
2 who is a good listener.
3 who sold me the torn skirt.
4 who performed marvellously in yesterday's match.
5 who stopped the fight between two classmates.

Practice E
1 She was the one who started the campaign.
2 He waved to his fans who were cheering for him.
3 This book is for everyone who wants to succeed.
4 She is filming farmers who are harvesting rice.
5 My dog barks at people who ride bicycles.

Practice F
2 Ted is one of the students who are organising the big walk.
3 Sally comforted a little boy who was crying for his mother.
4 The factory had two supervisors who were very strict.
5 An astronaut is a person who travels in a spacecraft.
6 It's Tim's idea so he is the one who has to explain.

16.4 SENTENCE STRUCTURE

Practice A

1 B	2 A	3 C	4 C	5 B

Practice B

1	who	2	which	3	loves	4	is	5	who
6	who is	7	which	8	eat	9	does	10	which

Practice C
1 which his father owns.
2 which I bought just now.
3 which is beside the park.
4 which is not too expensive.
5 which you made about her.

Practice D
1 which was landing.
2 who helped us.
3 who designed this building.
4 which came into our house.
5 which is near Bangkok.

Practice E
1 We read about the stolen diamonds which belonged to a rich banker.
2 My brother repaired our gate which fell off its hinges two days ago.
3 I watched the deer which were drinking at the pool.
4 James loves the carpentry set which was a gift from his grandfather.
5 Sue leapt up and caught the balloon which was floating in the air.

Practice F

1	…which live nearby.	→ who
2	…blocking her view.	→ is blocking
3	…who have very keen members.	→ which
4	…making us feel tired all the time.	→ was making
5	…which were flying kites.	→ who

Practice G
1 That team has players who are among the best in the world.
2 These are machines which will change our lives and this is the scientist who invented them.
3 I know a college which is conducting / conducts very useful courses. They help students gain skills which make them effective workers.
4 The mayor was staring at the fire which was destroying the city hall. His wife was thanking everybody who was helping to put out the fire.
5 Mum accidentally broke the bangle which was to be my birthday present. She gave me another bangle which was even more beautiful.

16.5 SENTENCE STRUCTURE

Practice A

1	because	4	jumping, excited	7	because of
2	because	5	because	8	torn
3	likes	6	pleased	9	early

Practce B
2 They won because they played well.
3 Adam shouted because he was angry.
4 I like flowers because they are beautiful.
5 We are fat because we love sweets.
6 The cat mewed because it was hungry.

Practice C
1 Mark did not have dinner because he was full.
2 Our old car runs well because we look after it.
3 My grandmother is excited because she is going on a holiday.
5 She was absent because she had a fever.

Practice D

1 B	2 A	3 A	4 B	5 A

Practice E
1 because its surroundings are beautiful.
2 because the accommodation is reasonable.
3 because the land is flat.
4 because they want to improve their game.
5 because the course is well-lit.

Practice F

1 A, B	2 C	3 A, B, C	4 A, B, C	5 B

Practice G

1	because	5	dirty	8	of
2	it's	6	passes	9	silly
3	don't	7	air	10	smart
4	is				

TEST 1

A

1	the	2	a	3	a	4	The	5	a
6	the	7	a	8	an	9	an	10	the

B

1 The ladies' committee decided to hold their food fair next week.
2 Mrs Tan's youngest grandchild is a chubby four-month-old boy.
3 The cheetah's long slender legs enable the animal to run at great speed.
4 My best friend's aunt is a well-known criminal lawyer.
5 The two lost sheep's bleats were heard by the shepherd.

C

1	He	2	His	3	It	4	wife	5	father

D

1	C	2	A	3	C	4	D	5	D
6	B	7	D	8	B	9	A	10	A

E

1	intent	5	most surprised	8	triumphant
2	red white large	6	better	9	bright
3	deeply	7	loud	10	joyful
4	black big				

F

1	work	5	doesn't	8	Does
2	are renovating	6	don't	9	Do
3	isn't	7	Is	10	Is
4	doesn't				

TEST 2

A

1 Rabbits are very cute animals.
2 They hid the stolen goods here.
3 You have to write a letter of thanks to your host.
4 Dad and I play volleyball every Sunday.
5 I found a silver bracelet under the sofa.
6 The dogs are barking furiously at a stranger.
7 Jonathan is a very active child.
8 Everyone is to be here on time.
9 Janet and I are learning Spanish.
10 Brian's latest painting is excellent.

B

1	am sitting	5	will be	8	had to fly
2	has	6	feel	9	am
3	know	7	was to meet	10	is
4	is coming				

C

1	kneads	5	shrieked	8	are packing
2	is	6	dropped	9	will be boarding

3	was taking	7	knelt	10	are going to
4	went				

D

1	aren't we	2	isn't it	3	aren't you
4	aren't I	5	isn't she		

E

1	When	2	does	3	Whose	4	did, leave

F

1 They hunted wild horses solely for food in prehistoric times.
2 They ploughed fields, carried goods, rounded up cattle and transported people from place to place.
3 Soldiers used horses in wartime.
4 Bucephalus died after a battle in 326 BC.
5 Caligula's horse held a position in the Roman Senate.

TEST 3

A

1	–	2	on	3	At	4	in	5	beside
6	on	7	at	8	in	9	beside	10	–

B

1 My uncle and aunt are interior decorators.
2 Why didn't you return my phone call?
3 John's sketch of the river is excellent.
4 Those aren't the chairs I ordered from your store.
5 My mother's not free to come to the phone right now.

C

1	Can	2	can	3	Can anyone
4	may	5	rent		here

D

1   2   5   6   10

E

1 The village had a rowing team which won several races.
2 We remember her because her drama classes were delightful.
3 Jane is a circus trainer who teaches elephants to dance.
4 My neighbour says his plants grow well because he talks to them.
5 He is the captain of the ship which will sail to India tonight.
6 Mr Hall is the architect who designed my neighbour's bungalow.
7 She didn't get the job because she didn't have the necessary qualifications.
8 This is the vacuum cleaner which is the lightest and most efficient in the market.
9 Please point out the sales assistant who was discourteous to you.
10 All of us love the song which made Rick Jones a singing sensation overnight.

F

1 It is especially hard for my family because of we all like different things. → It is especially hard for my family because we all like different things.
2 My father is a person he needs a lot of space. → My father is a person who needs a lot of space.

3 It is easy to keep clean because she wants one. → She wants one because it is easy to keep clean.

4 He would like a house like his friend's who looks really striking. → He would like a house like his friend's which looks really striking.

5 My dream house is one of those cottages which is found in the countryside. → My dream house is one of those cottages which are found in the countryside.

TEST 4

A

1	Its	2	lives	3	eats / catches	4	see	5	its
6	it	7	its	8	kingfishers	9	is	10	The

B

1 The writer's / His ambition is to sail solo around the world before he reaches the age of 40.

2 He is 15 (years old) now.

3 The writer's father taught him about boating.

4 He started a fund last year / in December last year / last December.

5 He goes around the neighbourhood to get odd jobs.

C

1	C	5	A	9	D	13	B	17	D
2	B	6	C	10	B	14	C	18	C
3	C	7	D	11	A	15	A	19	B
4	B	8	C	12	D	16	D	20	A

D

1 That is the motorist who dented Dad's car.

2 Celia came home late because of the heavy rain.

3 John can cook but he prefers to eat out.

4 Here are the notes which Larry misplaced.

5 The meeting ended late because there was so much to decide.

TEST 5

A

1	It	5	consists	8	and / while
2	is	6	The	9	has / uses
3	a / his / the	7	ones / squares	10	who
4	in				

B

1 They own two shops.

2 They leave their house at 6 a.m.

3 They go to their shops every morning.

4 They go there by van.

5 He carries boxes of things and arranges them on the shelves before the shops open.

C

1	C	5	A	9	A	13	D	17	C
2	A	6	B	10	D	14	D	18	D
3	B	7	C	11	D	15	A	19	B
4	B	8	B	12	A	16	C	20	C

D

1 Alan fell in the canteen because the floor was slippery. / Alan fell because the floor in the canteen was slippery.

2 We chased the man who snatched Lily's handbag.

3 Our coach cancelled the tennis practice because he was ill.

4 The zebra didn't see the leopards which were on the tree.

5 Ann and her sister like dancing but their brother hates it.

TEST 6

A

1	we	5	who	8	teachers
2	students	6	They	9	but
3	They	7	games	10	on
4	the				

B

1 She was at the river that morning.

2 She couldn't go to school because her parents could not afford it.

3 A well-dressed man asked Anita for directions to the school.

4 It fell out of his pocket.

5 He visited Anita's parents a month later.

C

1	B	5	B	9	A	13	C	17	B
2	D	6	C	10	A	14	D	18	B
3	B	7	C	11	D	15	C	19	D
4	A	8	C	12	A	16	A	20	D

D

1 You and I have to sit for five papers.

2 I am rather untidy, aren't I?

3 That is the man who tutors my brothers.

4 Everyone listens to him because he is sensible.

5 They followed the trail which led to the quarry.